FEASTS and FASTS
of ISRAEL

*An Account of Religious Customs in Jewish
Homes and Synagogues of To-day*

By

AARON JUDAH KLIGERMAN

Director, Emmanuel Neighborhood House

With an Introduction

By

WALTER LEE LINGLE

President of Davidson College

Published by the
Emmanuel Neighborhood House
*2102 E. Baltimore, St.,
Baltimore, Md.*
1931

Second Edition

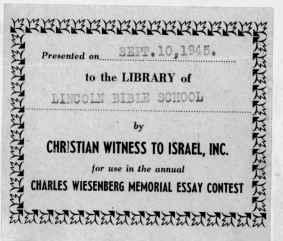

DEDICATED TO

HOWARD A. KELLY, M. D.

A scientist, a true follower of
the Messiah, a lover of Israel,
and an inspiration to the author

Feasts and Fasts of Israel

AARON JUDAH KLIGERMAN

CONTENTS

Introduction

The author of this little book is a Jew. He is also a Christian. These two facts qualify him to interpret the Jewish religion to Christian people, and at the same time interpret the Christian religion to the Jewish people. That is precisely what he has done in this book. He has pointed out to the Jews how the Christ of the New Testament was fore-shadowed by the sacrifices, feasts and fasts of the Old Testament. Even more fully he has shown to the Christians the present state of religion among the Jewish people. This is something which very few Christians know. Here we have described all the feasts and fasts which are observed by the orthodox Jews today.

I can commend the book to Christians and Jews alike. It will enable them to understand each other better in the realm of religion. In the book one can feel that the heart of the author yearns over his own people. He can say with the Apostle Paul: "I could wish that myself were accursed from Christ for my brethren, my kinsman according to the flesh." He is pouring out his life in their behalf.

Walter L. Lingle

Davidson College,
North Carolina.

Preface

These chapters are written with a view to increasing the Christian reader's knowledge of the Jews, and to stimulating his interest in their spiritual welfare.

It is their endeavor to emphasize the close but often obscured relationships between Judaism and Christianity, to tell Christians of the religious life of the Jews in America today, to give a concise account of the significance of the feasts and fasts of Israel, and of methods of observing these employed by Jews in our midst; and in these ways to increase Christians' understanding of the Jewish people, and to enlist a deeper devotion to their spiritual needs.

For the information that the book contains, the author is indebted not only to his own Jewish birth and training, or to his experience of eighteen years as a Christian worker among the Jews, but also to many original Hebrew sources and to a considerable number of authorities on Jewish history, life and customs.

My special desire is through these pages to advance the glory of God and to arouse prayerful concern in behalf of my brethren according to the flesh, the kinsmen of our Lord Jesus Christ, "who are Israelites; to whom pertaineth the adoption, and the glory, and the covenants, and the giving of the law, and the service of God, and the promises; whose are the fathers." Yet more than this: "Of whom as concerning the flesh Christ came, who is over all, God blessed forever" (ROMANS 9:3-5).

Aaron Judah Kligerman.

Rosh Hashonah, 5691
Baltimore, Maryland

I

"OF WHOM CHRIST CAME"

TO the Christian it is most impressive, and it hardly can be less so to the Jew, to observe how intimate and enlightening are many of the inter-relations between the Christian Church and the history, rites and customs of the Jewish religion. Great significance lies in the general recognition of Christianity as the direct and logical development of Jewish life and history as recorded in the Old Testament. When the Christian thus looks on his New Testament as nothing else than the fulfillment of the Old, when he sees the Lord Jesus Christ, Son of David, as He of whom Moses and the Prophets did speak, he has reason to have at least a dim sense of close kinship with Israel. He is, in fact, a spiritual brother of the Jew of to-day, as well as his ancestors of Israel's ancient past.

A vivid illustration of that spiritual relationship is afforded by the deeper implications of the lives of many characters of Old Testament history. In particular, their foreshadowing of the Christ of Christianity is quite as momentous as its repeated emphasis by Christian writers suggests. Just as Adam was the first of the human family, so Jesus Christ is emphasized as the first of God's new kingdom upon earth. As Abraham was the father of the faithful, Jesus Christ is his Son, He in whom each family of the earth is blessed. Of neither the birth nor death of Melchizedek, priest and king, has any record been found; he foreshadowed Jesus Christ, Son of God living forever to make intercession for us. Aaron was the high priest of the Old Covenant, Jesus the true High Priest of the New, who has gone behind the veil and entered the Holiest in the Heavens. Moses, the ideal law giver of old, founded the commonwealth of Israel and led the people through Red sea and wilderness, but Christ, as Founder of a new and spiritual Kingdom of Israel, is leading His people through waters of temptation till at last they reach the true and heavenly Canaan---their Promised Land.

Of scarcely less vital meaning to the Christian are the festivals of Israel. Most of these - and certainly the most significant of them - obviously hark back to that Testament of thirty-nine books which is an essential part of the Christian's Bible. It would be difficult to remain a while in any modern synagogue during the ceremonies of such a great day as the Day of Atonement, without constantly thinking of Old Testament heroes of the faith. The Feasts of Tabernacles, of Lots and of Trumpets also place one in the atmosphere of Bible thought and experience. As for the Passover Feast, its close relationship to the entire Christian plan of redemption, from the sin of our first parents to the triumphant death on Calvary, is abundantly clear.

A description of these significant Jewish festivals is considered likely to bring some new light to Christians not intimately acquainted with them. It is also reasonable to hope that this proposed visit to Jewish Ghetto, home and synagogue will lead to at least three additional results. It may add to the Christian reader's knowledge of Old Testament teachings and customs, as seen against the background of modern Jewish life. It may increase his understanding of that Jewish life of to-day, and arouse

16

a deeper sympathy with the modern people of Israel. Again, this view of Jewish customs may serve to emphasize the one all-important fact—that the Jew of to-day, however devoted he may be to the details of his religious festivals, is in grievous need of the Gospel of Christ Jesus.

II

THE FEAST OF REDEMPTION

Passover

The Passover of the Jews is a symbol of the Redemption in Christ Jesus. Of the three names by which this feast is known - *Hag ha Matzoth*, "the Feast of Unleavened Bread"; *Zeman Herusanau*, "the Season of Our Freedom"; and *Pesach*, "Passed Over" - the last one is most often used. The reference is to the account in Exodus, chapter twelve, of how, when the angel of death killed the first-born of the Egyptians, he "passed over" the homes inhabited by the children of Israel, each of which had been carefully marked with a sprinkling of lamb's blood on the doorposts.

Readers of the New Testament are quick to note the significance of the lamb, the blood of which preserved Israel from death. The Redeemer is frequently mentioned in the New Testament under the emblem of a lamb. When the Baptist proclaims Him he says: "Behold the Lamb of God!" (JOHN 1:36). John speaks of Him as "the Lamb slain from the foundation of the world" (REVELATION 13:8); and Paul describes Him as "Christ our Passover, sacrificed for us: therefore let us keep the feast" (I CORINTHIANS 5:7, 8).

Many were the offerings presented during the Passover feast (see Numbers 28:11), but the special and most important one was the Paschal lamb (EXODUS 12:3). Regarding this central feature of the feast, at least six considerations were prominent and essential;

18

each one was to teach some truth concerning Him who is the "Lamb of God, which taketh away the sin of the world" (JOHN 1:29):

1. The Paschal lamb was required to be "without blemish" (EXODUS 12:5), a law which led the Jews of old to examine with a most rigid scrutiny each lamb destined to the altar. Simon Peter, referring to what transpired on Calvary, reminds us: "Ye know that ye were not redeemed with corruptible things, as silver and gold; but with the precious blood of Christ, as of a lamb without blemish and without spot" (I PETER 1:18, 19).

2. The Paschal lamb was selected from the flock. What fact could more clearly indicate the sameness of Messiah's human nature with that of those for whom He was to be offered? What better proof that He was in all things "made like unto His brethren" (HEBREWS 2:17)?

3. The Paschal lamb was to be killed in the evening (EXODUS 12:6), "between the evenings," [1] as the Hebrew text has it. Jesus, our Paschal Lamb, died "between the evenings." The suffering began at the third hour, 9 a. m. (MARK 15:25), and when the sixth hour came, 12 noon, darkness covered the whole land till the ninth hour, 3 p. m., the very hour of Israel's sacrificing the Passover lamb.

Footnote: 1. "The Samaritans and many modern interpreters seem to think that this means between actual sunset and complete darkness (or say between 6 and 7 p m.) ; but from the contemporary testimony of Josephus, and from Talmudical authorities, there cannot be a doubt that, at the time of our Lord, it was regarded as the interval between the sun's commencing to decline and its actual disappearance. This allows a sufficient period for the numerous lambs which had to be killed, and agrees with the traditional account that on the eve of the Passover the daily evening sacrifice was offered an hour, or, if it fell on a Friday, two hours before the usual time."—David Baron in *Types, Psalms, and Prophecies.*

4. The blood of the Paschal lamb was sprinkled upon the side posts and upper doorpost of each Jewish home (EXODUS 12:7). The apostle Peter in one of his letters uses the very term used in Exodus: "Elect according to the foreknowledge of God the Father, through sanctification of the Spirit, unto obedience and sprinkling of the blood of Jesus Christ" (I PETER 1:2).

5. The Paschal lamb was to be consumed the night it was killed; nothing was to be left for the next day (EXODUS 12:10). The body of Jesus, our Paschal Lamb, was not left on the cross over night. His crucifixion took place on the fourteenth of Nisan, the preparation day for the Sabbath: "The Jews therefore, because it was the preparation, besought Pilate that their legs might be broken, and that they might be taken away" (JOHN 19:31). Pilate gave orders for the removal of the bodies, and all the three crucified were taken down.

6. Not one bone of the Paschal lamb was to be broken (EXODUS 12:46); no bone of Jesus' body was broken. When the soldiers came to the bodies of the thieves, but found them still alive, they broke the men's legs in order to hasten death. But when they came to the body of Jesus, ready to treat Him in the same manner, they found Him already dead (JOHN 19:33). Yet to make more certain of it, they pierced His side with a sword (JOHN 19:34). (See PSALM 22:16, 17).

When our Lord Jesus used certain words about Himself which were not understood at that time—"Except ye eat the flesh of the Son of man, and drink his blood, ye have no life in you"—it was the Passover of which He was thinking. After his sacrifice on Calvary, His followers were to have a new Passover. He became their Passover Lamb: "Behold the Lamb of God, which taketh away the sin of the world." The bread at the Com-

20

munion table, He told His disciples, represents His body, and the wine His blood. By solemnly eating this bread and drinking this wine in remembrance of Him, they would be partaking of the new spiritual Passover.

With the destruction of the Temple in 70 A. D., all sacrifices connected with the Temple ceased. The Rabbis, nevertheless, seeking to create substitute means of emphasizing and strengthening Israel's hope of another redemption, in later times composed the *Haggadah*, a ritual which they built on the "Tale of Passover" and which they ordained to be observed in the Jewish home. This Rabbinical way of keeping the Passover, which is followed by multitudes of Jews to-day, is described in the following paragraphs.

Weeks before the Passover, unleavened cakes are made, in quantities large enough to supply the place of the bread used in the home at other times. The *matzos* are commonly round and thin and are full of tiny holes. They are composed of flour and water only; the reason only "unleavened bread" is to be eaten during the Passover is stated in DEUTERONOMY 16:3. The Israelites were to remember that "thou camest forth out of the land of Egypt in haste." It is "the bread of affliction."

On the thirteenth day of the month Nisan (March or April), in the morning, the most careful and minute inquisition is made by the head of each family. He searches every part of his house, in order to clear it of leavened bread and of every other particle of leaven, *chametz*. All that is discovered is collected in a vessel, and, together with the vessel in which it is deposited, is solemnly burned before noon the next day. Obviously this custom involves a difficulty for merchants who own establishments in which considerable leaven is on hand. In many such cases, if it is not easy to remove the leaven, the owner sells his store to a Gentile, giving him the keys, with a written agreement that the store shall be returned to him at the end of seven days.

On the fourteenth day of the month the first-born son of each family is required to fast. This he does in remembrance of the protection enjoyed by the first-born of Israel at the time when God smote all the first-born of the Egyptians. On the evening of the same day the men assemble in the synagogue to usher in the festival by prayers, as is prescribed in the ritual.

It is customary to honor *Seder,* the home Passover festival, by an exhibition of the most sumptuous furniture that the home can afford.) The table is covered with a clean linen cloth. On the cloth are laid several plates. On one plate there are placed the following articles: The "shank bone" of a shoulder of lamb or kid, commemorative of the Passover lamb; a roasted egg, a substitute for the ancient holiday sacrifice, *Korban Chagigah;* a root of horse-radish, *maror,* symbol of the bitterness endured under the Egyptians; some parsley, *karpas;* and a compound of ground apples, almonds and raisins, mixed with wine, *charoseth,* representing the bricks which our forefathers were required to make. On another plate three *matzos,* unleavened cakes, are carefully wrapped in a napkin. These represent the priest and Levite and the Israelite—symbolizing the threefold division of the Jewish people.

The family being seated, the king of the house (every Jewish father is a "king" on the first two nights of the Passover week) pronounces grace over the table in general, and over the wine in particular. Then, leaning in a stately manner on his left arm, an indication of liberty, he drinks a glass of wine. All other members of the household follow his example. After the wine he

22

dips some of the herbs in the vinegar and eats, repeating another benediction.

The head of the house next unfolds the napkin and, taking the middle cake, breaks it in two. One half of it he leaves lying with the two other cakes, and conceals the second half beneath his cushion as he reclines at the table. This concealed half-cake is called *afikoman*, in professed allusion to the circumstances recorded by Moses that "the people took their dough before it was leavened, their kneading troughs being bound up in their clothes" (EXODUS 12:34).

Now he removes the shank bone and egg from the table. Then, while the head of the house holds up the plate with the cakes, the whole household unites in repeating:

"This is the bread of poverty and affliction which our fathers did eat in Egypt. Whosoever hungers, let him come and eat. Whosoever needs, let him come and eat of the Paschal lamb. This year we are here; the next, God willing, we shall be in the land of Israel. This year we are servants; the next, if God wills, we shall be as free men." [2]

The shank bone and egg are again placed on the table. Another glass of wine is taken, and the time has arrived for the smallest child to ask questions. If no children are present some adult puts the questions. Their nature is suggested by the following question and replies:

1. "Wherefore is this night distinguished from all other nights?" Any other night we may eat either leavened or unleavened bread, but on this night only unleavened bread."

2. "Any other night we may eat any species of herb, but this night only bitter herbs."

Footnote: 2. *The Standard Haggadah,* by H. E. Goldin.

3. "Any other night we do not dip (the vegetables) even once; on this night, we have to dip them twice."

4. "On all other nights we eat and drink either sitting or leaning, but on this night we all lean." [3]

The answers to the questions take in nearly the whole story of Israel's history, from the calling of Abraham from "the other side of the flood" to the people's redemption from Egyptian bondage. The questioning is followed by Psalms and hymns.

Pieces of *matzos* are distributed among the members of the household, and now instead of the Paschal lamb the family eats this unleavened bread, seasoning it with some of the bitter herbs and part of the thick paste *charoseth* in memory of the bricks made in Egypt. But the oblation of the Paschal lamb has been wholly discontinued.

A plentiful supper follows, with two more glasses of wine; for the Jews are required to drink on this occasion four glasses of wine each. The fourth and last glass is accompanied by the repetition of certain passages from the Scripture, imprecating divine vengeance on the heathen and on all the enemies of Israel. There is a special cup, filled with wine, called *Kos shel Elijahu*, the cup of the prophet Elijah, who, according to Jewish legend, visits every *Seder* and who, at the end of days will bring tidings of the coming of Messiah.

The concluding ceremony of the *Seder* service is the singing of *"Chad Gadya,"* a children's song whose title may be translated, "An Only Kid." Until a few years ago many persons believed that *"Chad Gadya"* was more than a children's song, many books indeed were written to explain the supposed meaning of the series of events begun when "Daddy bought one only kid." The favorite

---

Footnote: 3. *The Standard Haggadah,* by H. E. Goldin.

interpretation of the song was that "the only kid" represents the people of Israel, that the father who bought the kid is God, and that the two pieces of gold represent Moses and Aaron, for it was through them that God redeemed Israel from Egypt. The animals and objects that come upon the scene were regarded as symbolizing different oppressors from whom Israel suffered in the course of its long history. These are the words of "Chad Gadya":

A kid my father bought
For two *zuzim*—
An only kid, an only kid.

Then came the cat [Assyria], and ate the kid
That my father bought
For two *zuzim*—
An only kid, an only kid.

Then came the dog [Babylonia], and bit the cat
That ate the kid
That my father bought
For two *zuzim*—
An only kid, an only kid.

Then came the stick [Medio-Persia], and beat the dog
That bit the cat that ate the kid
That my father bought
For two *zuzim*—
An only kid, an only kid.

Then came the fire [Macedonia], and burned the stick
That beat the dog that bit the cat that ate the kid
That my father bought
For two *zuzim*—
An only kid, an only kid.

Then came the water [Rome], and quenched the
fire

That burned the stick

That beat the dog that bit the cat that ate the kid

That my father bought

For two *zuzim*—

An only kid, an only kid.

Then came the ox [the Saracens], and drank the
water

That quenched the fire that burned the stick

That beat the dog that bit the cat that ate the kid

That my father bought

For two *zuzim*—

An only kid, an only kid.

Then came the butcher [the Crusaders], and slew
the ox

That drank the water that quenched the fire

That burned the stick that beat the dog

That bit the cat that ate the kid

That my father bought

For two *zuzim*—

An only kid, an only kid.

Then came the Angel of Death [the Turk], and
killed the butcher

That slew the ox that drank the water that
quenched the fire

That burned the stick that beat the dog that bit
the cat

That ate the kid that my father bought

For two *zuzim*—

An only kid, an only kid.

Then came the Holy One [God], and killed the
Angel of Death that slew the butcher

That slew the ox that drank the water
That quenched the fire that burned the stick
That beat the dog that bit the cat that ate the kid
That my father bought
For two *zuzim*—
An only kid, an only kid. [4]

A custom worthy of note, which begins immediately after the evening service on the eve before the second day of Passover and continues seven weeks, until the Feast of Weeks, is the "counting of the *omer*." The *omer*, a measure about the size of a half-gallon, contained the sample of the first harvest which every pilgrim brought as an offering to the priest when he came to Jerusalem on this feast. The institution of counting, or *sefirah*, is based on the following verses from LEVITICUS 23:15, 16:

"And ye shall count unto you from the morrow after the sabbath, from the day that ye brought the sheaf of the wave offering; seven sabbaths shall be complete: even unto the morrow after the seventh sabbath shall ye number fifty days."

During this period of *sefirah* days Jews neither marry nor give banquets; it is a season of sadness. Instead, they recall the days of the unsuccessful uprising of Bar Kochba (125 A. D.) against the Roman yoke when so large a number of their brethren were killed. According to tradition many of Israel's great men were massacred during these sad years. There is, however, one day during the seven weeks when joyous occasions may be celebrated, the thirty-third day of the *Omer*. Tradition states that the plague which raged among the disciples of Rabbi Akibah was stayed on this day. There-

---

Footnote: 4. From the *Union Home Study Magazine*.

fore, the one temporary break in the weary season of sadness.

To one who has participated in the orthodox observance of the Passover with its climax of utter sorrow, there is deep consolation in many a prophetic word from the Jewish Scriptures. For him and for the Jews whose every Passover brings desolate mourning, abundant hope lies in such a declaration as that of ISAIAH 61:3. The Lord hath indeed sent "unto them that mourn in Zion" One whose compassionate desire is "to give unto them beauty for ashes, the oil of joy for mourning, the garment of praise for the spirit of heaviness."

When once His love has had its way, then will there come to Israel not a temporary interruption but a complete ending of its Passover season of sadness.

III

THE FEAST OF WEEKS
Shabuoth

On the sixth day of the third month, called Sivan, which is the fiftieth of the *omer,* Jews celebrate a feast which according to DEUTERONOMY 16:10 is called "The Feast of Weeks." This feast is described also as "The Feast of Harvest" (EXODUS 23:16) and as "The Day of the First Fruits" (NUMBERS 28:26), because an offering was then made of two loaves, the produce of the corn just reaped. This festival, now kept for two days, is observed with the same strictness as the first two days of Passover.

A peculiar service at the synagogue is a feature of the celebration of the Feast of Weeks. In certain parts of Europe it is customary to adorn not only the synagogues but also the houses with green leaves and flowers. The book of Ruth is read at the synagogue, because the circumstances it relates took place at the time of the harvest. At this time, too, the Jews maintain, the Law was delivered on Mount Sinai, *Zeman-matton Torathenu,* and therefore that portion of Scripture which tells of the delivery of the decalogue is solemnly read. The special lessons are these: First day—EXODUS 19, 20, the giving of the Law on Sinai; EZEKIEL 1, the revelation of God's glory. Second day—DEUTERONOMY 15:19; 16:17; Habakkuk 3.

In many places the night preceding the Feast of Weeks also is observed in the synagogue, by a watch during which the 613 precepts, said to comprehend the whole Law, are recited. This institution had its origin in the three days' preparation enjoined upon ancient Israel to sanctify the people for receiving the Law (EXODUS 19:10-12).

To the Christian the Feast of Weeks has a very definite meaning. Once in Jerusalem, when a number of disciples of Jesus were met to pray, a remarkable effusion of the Holy Spirit was given to them. From this time forth they were aware that times of refreshing had come to them, and in the inspiration of their new joy they went out into the world to do their work victoriously as messengers of Jesus. That marvelous gift of the Holy Spirit was poured out at the time of the Feast of Weeks—Pentecost.

The wonderful occurrences of the day of Pentecost, as related in ACTS 2, were the fulfillment of the prophecy of Joel, one of the earliest of the early prophets sent to call his people to repentance. In the midst of national calamity he had pointed out the necessity of a return to God, and had delivered gracious promises of spiritual blessings upon the people if they should repent. There is every reason to believe that his ministry was in fact attended by a widespread religious revival. But Joel had also promised that God's Spirit would be poured out not only upon Israel but upon all flesh, and that spiritual and gracious blessings like those he had foretold for his own people would attend such widespread effusion of the Spirit.

Pentecost fulfilled that promise. Unlettered and provincial men were transformed on that day into eloquent expounders of the deep yet simple doctrines of the cross. Men who before had been fearful and unbelieving now became fearless. They boldly charged the death of Jesus to its real authors, but at the same time they opened the gates of repentance and of mercy to these very men. It was they who plainly declared to the whole house of Israel that there is no salvation in any other name than the name of Jesus.

To the Christian Hebrew, Pentecost is an indisputable proof—and let it be such to every Christian—that the Jew can be won to Christ. Pentecost won Jews to Him. The Gospel which He had preached and lived, and which the apostles preached after Him, on that ever memorable occasion turned three thousand to Him, including a multitude of Jews. As long as the record of that day stands, an unanswerable argument faces any Christian who, in unconscious opposition to the Spirit of God, asserts: "There is no use in preaching to the Jews." Let us avoid such words.

Instead, let us all thus pray: "O God, who as at this time didst teach the hearts of thy faithful people, by sending to them the light of Thy Holy Spirit: grant us by the same Spirit to have a right judgment in all things, and evermore to rejoice in his holy comfort; through the merits of Christ Jesus our Saviour, who liveth and reigneth with thee, in the unity of the same Spirit, one God, world without end."

IV

A DAY OF MOURNING
Tisha B'av

A most unhappy day in Jewish history and experience is "Tisha B'av," the ninth day of the Jewish month Av, in July or August. On this ninth day of Av both the Temples were destroyed, the first in 586 B. C., by the Babylonians under Nebuchadnezzar, the second in 70 A. D., by the Romans under Titus. From Titus' time to now great have been the sufferings of Israel. Her sons have wandered afar and as yet have found no resting place. Their lot has been to live in segregated Ghettos. They have been massacred by Crusaders; banished from lands in which for a while they tarried in prosperity; forced to wear distinctive badges; compelled to suffer multiplied indignities. Restrictive laws have been passed against them, false accusations heaped upon their heads. In our own day their situation in many lands is one of bitterness and accumulated sorrow.

To commemorate the sad events of the past, to mourn with their brethren who are still suffering, and to pray for the restoration of their Home Land, this is the purpose of the Day of Mourning. As a matter of fact, it is the conclusion of "the three weeks" of mourning during which time no festivity, no wearing of new clothes, no weddings, no dedications of new buildings is permissible. On the last nine days preceding the fast day, orthodox Jews refrain from eating meat, which at this time is a symbol of the sacrifices offered in the Temple, and also from bathing and listening to music.

On Tisha B'av the synagogues are filled with mourners. In a profoundly melancholy chant the scroll of Lamentations is read. When the verse "He hath set me in dark places, as they that be dead of old" (LAMENTATIONS 3:6) is reached all lights in the synagogue are suddenly extinguished. A solemn stillness prevails, Israel is mourning.

A long series of elegies, *kinoth,* is recited. Prominent among them is the "Ode of Zion" by Jehudah Halevi:

Art thou not Zion, fain
To send forth greetings from thy sacred rock
Unto thy captive train,
Who greet thee as the remnants of thy flock?
Take thou on every side,
East, west, south and north, their greetings mul-
    tiplied.
Sadly he greets thee still,
The prisoner of hope who, day and night,
Sheds ceaseless tears, like dew on Hermon's hill.
Would that they fell upon the mountain's height!

Harsh is my voice when I bewail thy woes,
But when in fancy's dreams
I see thy freedom, forth its cadence flows,
Sweet as the harps that hung by Babel's streams.
The glory of the Lord will ever be
Thy sole and perfect light;
No need hast thou, then, to illumine thee
Of sun by day, or moon and stars by night.
I would that, where God's spirit was of yore
Poured out into thy holy ones, I might
There too my soul outpour!

Oh, who will lead me on
To seek the spots where, in far distant years,
The angels in their glory dawned upon

Thy messengers and seers?
Oh, who will give me wings
That I may fly away,
And there, at rest from all my wanderings,
The ruins of my heart among thy ruins lay?
I'll bend my face unto thy soil, and hold
Thy stones as special gold.
And when, in Hebron, I have stood beside
My fathers' tombs, then will I pass in turn
Thy plains and forests wide,
Until I stand on Gilead, and discern
Mount Hor and Mount Abarim, 'neath whose crest
Thy luminaries twain, thy guides and beacons, rest.
Thy air is life unto my soul, thy grains
Of dust are myrrh, thy streams with honey flow—
Naked and barefoot to thy ruined fanes
How gladly would I go,
To where the ark was treasured, and in dim
Recesses dwelt the holy cherubim!

Perfect in beauty, Zion, how in thee
Do love and grace unite!
The souls of thy companions tenderly
Turn unto thee; thy joy was their delight,
And weeping they lament thy ruin now.
In distant exile, for thy sacred height
They long, and towards thy gates in prayer they
    bow.
Shinar and Pathros! come they near to thee?
Nought are they by thy light and right divine.
To what can be compared the majesty
Of thy annointed line?
To what the singers, seers and Levites thine?
The rule of idols fails and is cast down;
Thy power eternal is, from age to age thy crown.

The Lord desires thee for His dwelling place
Eternally, and bless'd
Is he whom God has chosen for the grace
Within thy courts to rest.
Happy is he that watches, drawing near,
Until he sees thy glorious lights arise,
And over whom thy dawn breaks full and clear,
Set in the Orient skies.
But happiest he who, with exultant eyes,
The bliss of thy redeemed ones shall behold,
And see thy youth renewed as in days of old! [1]

For almost nineteen hundred years Israel has been
in mourning. She has lamented over her loss of a national and spiritual center. Annually, daily, she has expressed her deep sorrow over this calamity. Her fasting
and her prayers have centered in a sad hope for an even-
tual rebuilding of the Temple at Jerusalem. To-day she
still cries aloud for the restoration of Zion. That restoration, let it indeed come. But would that my people
could see the secret of its coming! Let us all make haste
to turn our eyes unto Jesus, our own Messiah, and so
speed the day of our restoring.

It has been promised unto us: "If ye be willing and
obedient, ye shall eat the good of the land" (ISAIAH
1:19). These eyes of ours shall yet gaze upon a re-estab-
lished Zion: "Thine eyes shall see Jerusalem a quiet habi-
tation, a tabernacle that shall not be taken down"
(ISAIAH 33:20). And some day we shall even see Israel
counted a joy and blessing wherever man is found: "I
will give thee for a light to the Gentiles, that thou may-

Footnote: 1. Translation by Alice Lucas. Jehudah Halevi was
born in Old Castile in 1086 and is called "The Poet of Israel's
Golden Age." "His love for Jerusalem became his one controlling
passion. It colored all his thinking, and made him wretched in
the land of his birth" (Lewis Browne, in *Stranger Than Fiction*).

est be my salvation unto the end of the earth" (ISAIAH 49:6; *cf.* GENESIS 12:13).

The Lord hasten that day of Israel's restoration— and Israel, may she herself hasten!

V
THE FEAST OF TRUMPETS
Rosh Hashonah

The summer is now nearly gone. The seven mourning weeks *Sefira*, and the month of Av with its sorrowful "three weeks," are taking their departure. Soon will come the time of festivals and celebration, days of joy and holiness.

This is the beginning of the season during which the religious emotions of the Jew find their highest expression. The Feast of Trumpets, or New Year, to use the traditional [1] and most familiar name of the festival, falls on the first of Tishri [2] (September), the seventh month of the Hebrew year. According to Exodus 12:2, Nisan was regarded as the "head" of the year, the beginning "of the months." But the year, that is the civil or social year, actually began with Tishri. The name "New Year" is not found in the Bible, and in only one place (EZEKIEL 40:1) does the Hebrew expression *rosh hashonah* occur. The Scriptural titles of this festival are:

Footnotes:1. According to the *Mishna,* "Rosh Hashonah."

2. The first of Tishri is generally regarded by the Rabbis as the beginning of creation. The *Mishna* speaks of it especially as a day of judgment, on which all the children of men pass for judgment before the Creator, as sheep pass examination before the shepherd. Three books, says the Talmud, are open on Rosh Hashonah before the Creator, wherein the fate of the wicked, the righteous, and those of an intermediate class are recorded. The names of the righteous are immediately inscribed, and they are at once sealed "to life"; the middle class are allowed ten days, till the day of Atonement, to repent and become righteous; while the wicked are at once blotted out of "the book of the living."—ROSH-HASHONAH 1:2; 16b, *Mishna.*

"The memorial of Blowing Trumpets" (LEVITICUS 23:24) and "the Day of Blowing the Horn," *yom teruah,* according to NUMBERS 29:1.

The name *teruah,* the Scriptural name of the festival, reminds the Jew—according to the Jewish commentator Saadya—of the following ten features of national life, with each of which it is directly or indirectly connected:

1. The creation.
2. The duty to return to God.
3. The revelation on Mount Sinai.
4. The exhortations of the prophets.
5. The Destruction of the Temple.
6. The binding of Isaac for sacrifice.
7. Imminent danger.
8. The Day of Judgment.
9. The redemption of Israel.
10. The Resurrection.

That the horn or *shofar,* made of a ram's or wild goat's horn, rather than the trumpet of silver (NUMBERS 10:1-10), should have been designated as the instrument to be used during these "fearful days," is due perhaps to the impressive character of its note. In Biblical times the *shofar* was used for proclamations, especially on solemn occasions such as the Jubilee (LEVITICUS 25:9), and days of humiliation (JOEL 2:15), and also for sounding an alarm in time of war. Thus Amos (3:6) asks: "Shall a *shofar* be blown in the city, and the people not be afraid?" [3]

Footnote: 3. "Also to confuse Satan, for, at the hour in which Israel take their horns and sound before the Holy One, blessed be He, He rises from the throne of judgment and sits on the throne of mercy. He has pity upon them and changes the attribute of judgment which was against them, into mercy."— *Vayikra Rabbah,* section 29.

During the whole month of Elul—that is, for twenty-nine days before New Year—daily (except Saturdays) "Our Rabbis of blessed memory have ordained that this horn be blown" and "that Jews everywhere go upon the burial ground, in order that the dead should intercede in their behalf." [4] If distance separates them from the resting places of their departed relatives, they spare no pains to reach them. In passing the smallest cemetery in Europe, and even in civilized America, one may behold a multitude of both sexes and of every age prostrated upon the graves, offering prayers to the moldering remains of relatives, or favorite Rabbis, in the most lamentable strains.

One week before the Feast of Trumpets the Jews assemble in the synagogues, very early every morning for prayer and supplication. The day previous to the feast they again assemble for confession of sin and to remind God of His covenant with Abraham. This is the morning of *Zecher Brith,* a reminding of the covenant. According to the Rabbis, God says to Israel: "If you want to be declared innocent before me in judgment on this day [Rosh Hashonah], you must recall the merits of your fathers." [5]

For a similar purpose, on New Year's day there is recited in the synagogues the record of the binding of Isaac. God has mercy upon His creatures; He gives them a season for repentance, that they may not perish in their wickedness, for it is written (LAMENTATIONS 3:40) that we should "search and try our ways, and turn again to the Lord." The general expectation is that at this season, in which the original creation was accom-

Footnote: 4. *Taanith,* Fol. 16.

Footnote: 5. *Pesik.,* Bach. H. and Lev. R. 25.

plished, the re-creation or restitution of all things will take place. Much of the service of the day has direct reference to this subject. This hope is expressed in an affecting poem, sung immediately after the prayer for universal peace:

All the world shall come to serve Thee
    And bless Thy glorious Name,
And Thy righteousness triumphant
    The islands shall acclaim.

And the people shall go seeking
    Who knew Thee not before—
And the ends of earth shall praise Thee
    And tell Thy greatness o'er.

They shall build for Thee their altars,
    Their idols overthrown,
And their graven gods shall shame them,
    As they turn to Thee alone.

They shall worship Thee at sunrise
    And feel Thy kingdom's might,
And impart their understanding
    To those astray in night,

They shall testify Thy greatness
    And of Thy power speak,
And extol Thee, shrined, uplifted
    Beyond man's highest peak.

And with reverential homage,
    Of love and wonder born,
With the ruler's crown of beauty
    Thy head they shall adorn.

With the coming of Thy kingdom
    The hills shall break into song,
And the islands laugh exultant—
    That they to God belong.

And all their congregation
  So loud Thy praise shall sing
That the uttermost peoples, hearing,
  Shall hail Thee, crowned King. [6]

The *baltokia*, the one who blows the *shofar*, is standing in the center of the synagogue on an elevation, his prayer shawl drawn far over his head. Holding the curved instrument pressed gently to his lips, with all his power he makes the *shofar* sound clear and distinct.

While the *shofar* is being blown the following remarkably significant prayer is offered: "Merciful and gracious God, I have sinned against Thee, and done that which is evil in Thy sight. Have mercy on me and forgive all my transgressions, trespasses and sins, through Jesus, the Prince of His presence."

In most of the prayer books of the present day this prayer is omitted, and the following offered instead: "May it please Thee, O Lord God, and the God of our fathers, that the blowing of the *shofar* may come before Thee ... and that Thou mayest accept it as the mediation through Elijah and Joshua, the Prince of the Presence, the Prince Metatron [Messiah], and that Thou mayest be filled with mercy towards us. Blessed art Thou, O Lord who art merciful." [7]

The angel *Metatron*, according to Jewish theology, was he who discoursed with Moses (Exodus 3:2-15), and the angel in whom God placed His name. Though it is from the Latin, it expresses the same meaning as the Hebrew *Shadai*, as Rabbi Jarchi on Exodus 6:3 confesses. St. Jerome on Ezekiel 1:24 notes that the Greek

Footnote: 6. Translation from the Hebrew by Israel Zangwill, Jewish dramatist and author, author of *The Melting Pot, Dreamers of the Ghetto*, etc.

Footnote: 7. From *Prayers for New Year*.

interpreters sometime render God's name *Shadai* by Logos, which leads us to believe that the Jews of old considered *Shadai* and *Metatron* to be the same. [8]

The *shofar* is sounded three times. The first sound is called *malchioth*, or the Kingdom. It recognizes God as King and Creator of the Universe. To Him the Jew swears allegiance, and promises Him to be true to His plan, and to help to bring nearer the full realization of His Kingdom.

The second sound is called *zichroneth*, remembrances. This is to remind the Jew that God is not only King, but also Judge. And it is also to remind God of His promise made to Abraham, Isaac and Jacob, and to entreat Him to remember their posterity with mercy. Hence the following passage, added by Rab in the third century:

"Remember in our favor, O Lord our God, the oath which Thou hast sworn to our father Abraham on Mount Moriah; consider the binding of his son Isaac upon the altar when he suppressed his love in order to do Thy will with a whole heart! Thus may Thy love suppress Thy wrath against us, and through Thy great goodness may the heat of Thine anger be turned away from Thy people, Thy city and Thy heritage! . . . . Remember today in mercy in favor of his seed the binding of Isaac." [9]

Shofroth, trumpets, is the name of the third sound. Its purpose is to call God to remembrance of the time

Footnote: 8. Chullin 60:2; Jebamoth 16b: *Jewish Encyclopedia*, Vol. viii, 519. The following from the *Zohar* is of interest: "There is a Man, if a Man He is, who is an Angel. This Angel is *Metatron*, the Keeper of Israel; He is a man in the image of the Holy One, blessed be He, who is an Emanation from Him [from God]; yea, He [the *Metatron*] is Jehovah. Of Him cannot be said, He is created, formed or made; but He is the Emanation from God."—Zohar, Chapter 67, page 130.

Footnote: 9. *Jewish Encyclopedia*, Vol. 1., Page 303.

when He gave Israel the Law from Mount Sinai with the sound of the trumpet (EXODUS 19:19), and to invoke Him to hasten the time when the great trumpet shall be blown, "and they shall come which were ready to perish in the land of Assyria, and the outcasts in the land of Egypt, and shall worship the Lord in the holy mount at Jerusalem" (ISAIAH 27:13). The *Midrash* states it thus:

"Rabbi Levi said, 'Because Abraham, our father, had seen the ram extricating itself from one thicket and entangling itself in another, God said to Him: "Even thus will be the condition of thy children among the nations. They will become entangled in Babylon, afterwards in Persia; from Persia they will go to Greece, from Greece to Rome; but ultimately they will be redeemed by the horns of the ram'."

On the first day of this feast—or, when Rosh Hashonah falls on a Sabbath, on the second day—in the afternoon it is customary to go to the banks of a river, or to any other place where water is found, and to repeat the following while each person present shakes his garments over the water:

"Who is a God like unto Thee, that pardoneth iniquity and passeth by the transgressions of the remnant of his heritage? He restraineth not his anger forever, because he delighteth in loving kindness. He will turn again and have mercy upon us; He will subdue our iniquities. And Thou will cast their sins into the depths of the sea. O mayest Thou cast all the sins of Thy people, the house of Israel, into a place where they shall be no more remembered or visited, or even again come to mind. Thou wilt show faithfulness to Jacob, and loving kindness to Abraham, as Thou hast sworn to our fathers from days of old." [10]

43

Canon Kingsbury in his *Church and Synagogue* summerizes the New Year of the synagogue thus: "Rosh Hashonah is first a memorial of God's work of creation, accomplished (as believed) at this season. It proclaims the world's Creator as our King. It is, again, a memorial of the departure of the twelve tribes from Egypt, that great deliverance which is nevermore forgotten or omitted among the 'praises of Israel.' It is, further, a memorial of the giving of the Law on Sinai when 'the trumpet sounded long,' and a memorial also of the binding of Isaac, the patriarchal type of Him who 'humbled himself, becoming obedient even unto death, yea, the death of the cross' (PHIL. 2:8), imploring a renewal of that good will of the Heavenly Father which acts of faithful submission and obedience evoked on Mount Moriah.

"It is, finally, a memorial of the divinely promised return of Israel to Jerusalem in the latter days, the rebuilding of the Holy City, the long expected coming Messiah, and the glorious resurrection of the sleeping dead."

Footnote: 10. From *Prayers for New Year.*

VI
THE DAY OF ATONEMENT
Yom Kippur

The idea of Atonement is based upon a realizing sense of sin as a breaking away from God, and of the need of reconciliation with Him on the part of the soul that has sinned. Every sin—whether it be *het,* a straying away from the path of right, or *avon,* crookedness of conduct, or *pesha,* rebellious transgression—is a severance of the bond of life which unites the soul with its Maker. It is this feeling of estrangement from God that prompts the sinner to offer sacrifices. Hence the Day of Atonement.

The Day of Atonement, "Day of Coverings," is the only periodical fast appointed by the Mosaic law for national observance. "On the tenth day of this seventh month [Tishri, in September or October] there shall be a day of atonement: it shall be an holy convocation unto you; and ye shall afflict your souls, and offer an offering made by fire unto the Lord. And ye shall do no work in that same day: for it is a day of atonement, to make an atonement for you before the Lord your God. For whatsoever soul it be that shall not be afflicted in that same day, he shall be cut off from among his people. Ye shall do no manner of work: it shall be a statute for ever throughout your generations in all your dwellings. It shall be unto you a sabbath of rest [Lit, "A Sabbath of Sabbaths"], and ye shall afflict your souls: in the ninth day of the month at even, from even unto even, shall ye celebrate your sabbath" (LEVITICUS 23:27-32; cf. 16:29-31; NUMBERS 29:7).

On the Day of Atonement the sacrifices were three fold:

1. The ordinary daily sacrifices.
2. The peculiar expiatory sacrifices.
3. The festival sacrifices (NUMBERS 29:7-11).

Outstanding among the features of the day, however, was the presentation of the sin-offering by the high priest alone (LEVITICUS 16:33). For this purpose the high priest put off his glorious high-priestly garments, washed his body in water, and clad himself in simple linen vestments worn only on this occasion (LEVITICUS 16:4). Thus attired—that is, in the garments of humiliation; the white linen garments being distinguished from the more ornate garments, they would be recognized as a symbol of humiliation— the high priest proceeded with the special work of the day. This was, to "make an atonement for the holy sanctuary . . for the tabernacle of the congregation, and for the altar——for the priests, and for all the people of the congregation" (LEVITICUS 16:33).

The contrast between the Old and New Covenant developed in the Epistle to the Hebrews turns on just this point; that whereas the Jewish sanctuary had thus to be reconsecrated year by year, on the Day of Atonement, with the blood of the sin offerings of atonement, the Christian Church—that is, Christ's people—have been consecrated once and forever by His blood: "Christ was once offered to bear the sins of many" (HEBREWS 9:28). There is no need of repetition of His sacrificial work.

A witness to the imperfect and transitory character of the Old Dispensation was afforded by the repetition of consecrating sacrifices year by year. The same imperfection was evidenced by the ceremonies connected with the live goat, over which the sins of the people were confessed. The meaning of this ceremony has been pointed out by Dr. Edersheim: "The only meaning of which this seems really capable is, that though confessed guilt was removed from the people to the head of the goat, as the symbolical substitute, yet as the goat was not killed, only sent far away into 'a land not inhabited,' so, under the Old Covenant sin was not really blotted out, only put away from the people and put aside till Christ came; not only to take upon Himself the burden of transgression, but to blot it out and to purge it away." [1]

Although in God's own time Christ did come, "that he might sanctify the people with his own blood" (HEBREWS 13:12), Israel is still very far away from Him—and that in spite of its own great desire for reconciliation.

Very significant, as an evidence of the deep-rooted desire for some form of atonement sacrifice, is a certain custom known throughout Jewry today. On the eve before Atonement Day, a fowl is swung over one's head, while one solemnly pronounces it to be a vicarious sacrifice. The fowl is to be put to death in place of this Jew or Jewess, if perchance he is guilty of death because of sin.

In this general connection Jews read the following: "The children of men that sit in darkness and in the shadow of death, being bound in affliction and iron; he brought them out of darkness and the shadow of death, and brake their bands in sunder. Fools because of their

---

Footnote:1. *The Temple*, by Alfred Edersheim, Hebrew-Christian theologian and Bible teacher.

transgression, and because of their iniquities, are afflicted. Their soul abhorreth all manner of meat; and they draw near unto the gates of death. Then they cry unto the Lord in their trouble, and he saveth them out of their distresses. He sendeth his word, and healeth them from their destructions. Oh that man would praise the Lord for his goodness, and for his wonderful works to the children of men" (see Psalm 107:8-21). "If there be a messenger [angel] with him, as an interpreter [intercessor] one among a thousand to show unto man his uprightness: then he is gracious unto him, and saith, Deliver him from going down to the pit; I have found a ransom" (Job 33:23, 24).

Only a fowl is used in this ceremony; no other animal would serve. This is because of the Hebrew word for man. In Hebrew man is called *gever*. If *gever*, man, has sinned, *gever* must sustain the penalty of sin. But since the punishment is heavier than a man can bear, there is substituted for him a fowl, which in the Talmudical dialect is also *gever*. [2] *Gever* is sacrificed, and divine justice is satisfied.

Another custom, of similar character, is the receiving on the eve of Atonement Day, usually in the synagogue, of "forty stripes save one," as a penalty for one's sin in accordance with Deuteronomy 25:2. While the penitent is reciting the Confession of Sins the sexton, *shamus*, with gentle hand lays on the thirty-nine blows, using a whip of leather thongs.

After completion of the whipping and confession the family returns home for the last meal of the day. The Thanksgiving of this meal is "repeated in tears."

In the evening of the ninth of Tishri the public

Footnote: 2. *Midrash Rabba to Lam. III, 39; Kidd. 80b; Yoma I, 8.*

service of the Day of Atonement opens with a solemn and plaintive prayer-melody, *Kol Nidre*, All Vows. The cantor sings the words to a tune possessing such appealing beauty that in recent years it has become a favorite melody on the concert platform. Many persons have imagined the text of *Kol Nidre* to be a highly poetic prayer. In fact, however, it is only a dry legal formula written in the style of a prosaic lawyer:

"All vows and prohibitions, and bans, and devotions in sacrifice, and vowing by nickname [i. e., vows made in mutilated words], and penalties and oaths, which we have vowed, or which we have sworn, or which we have put under ban, or which we have forbidden to ourselves (from this day of Atonement to the next day of Atonement, may it come in peace); we have repented of all of them; let all of them be dissolved, abandoned, put at rest, be void, and be annulled, not valid, nor of force; our vows are no vows, our prohibitions are no prohibitions, our oaths are no oaths." [3]

First of five services on the Day of Atonement, this one which opens with *Kol Nidre* continues until 10 p. m. Many Jews remain in the synagogue for the whole night, reciting Psalms and offering special prayers. For our Rabbis say:

"At this time, when there is no Temple, and we have no altar, there is no atonement, but repentance. Repentance atones for all transgressions." [4]

On the next morning the people again meet in the synagogue expecting to remain until sundown. Most of the time is spent in repeating the prayers prepared by

Footnote: 3. From *Prayers for the Day of Atonement*.

Footnote: 4 From *Prayers for the Day of Atonement; Pesikta Shubah (ed Buber)*.

the Rabbis for the day. Of the numerous prayers used the following are a few illuminating examples:

"Oh, what shall we say in Thy presence, O thou who dwelleth above the universe? Or, what shall we declare unto Thee, who resideth above the skies? Knowest Thou not all the secret things, as well as the revealed?

"Thou knowest all the secrets of the world, and most hidden transactions of all living. Thou searchest all the inward parts, and examinest the reins and the heart so that there is nothing concealed from Thee, neither is anything hidden from Thy sight. Oh, may it then be acceptable in Thy presence, O Eternal, our God, and the God of our Fathers, to pardon all our sins, and forgive all our iniquities, and grant us remissions for all our transgressions.

"For the sin which we have committed against Thee, either by compulsion or voluntarily, and for the sin which we have committed against Thee with a stubborn heart.

"For the sin which we have committed against Thee out of ignorance, and for the sin which we have committed against Thee with the utterance of lips.

"For the sin which we have committed against Thee with incestuous lewdness, and for the sin which we have committed against Thee either publicly or secretly.

"For the sin which we have committed against Thee with deliberate deceit, and for the sin which we have committed against Thee with the speech of mouth.

"For the sin which we have committed against Thee by oppressing our neighbor, and for the sin which we committed against Thee by the evil cogitation of the heart.

"For the sin which we have committed against Thee by associating with impurity, and for the sin which we have committed against Thee by acknowledging our sin with our mouth (but do not repent in our heart).

"For the sin which we have committed against Thee by despising our parents and teachers, and for the sin which we have committed against Thee either through presumptuousness or ignorance.

"For the sin which we have committed against Thee with violence, and for the sin which we have committed against Thee by the profanation of Thy name.

"For the sin which we have committed against Thee with defiled lips, and for the sin which we have committed against Thee with foolish expressions.

"For the sin which we have committed against Thee either wittingly or unwittingly.

"Yet, for all of them, O God of forgiveness! forgive us, pardon us, and grant us remission.

"Also for the sins for which we were obliged to bring a burnt offering.

"And for the sins for which we were obliged to bring a sin offering.

"And for the sins for which we were obliged to bring an offering according to our ability.

"And for the sin for which we were obliged to bring a trespass offering, for either a certain or a doubtful sin.

"And for the sin for which we were obliged to suffer the stripes of contumacy.

"And for the sins for which we were obliged to suffer flagellation.

"And for the sin for which we have incurred the penalty of death from the hand of God.

"And for the sins for which we have incurred the punishment of excision, and being childless.

"And for all these, O God of forgiveness, forgive us, pardon us, grant us atonement." [5]

Prayers for the Day of Atonement include a memorial for the dead, *Hazkoras Neshamos*. It is the custom among all Jews to remember the souls of their departed parents on this great Day of Atonement, and on the closing days of the three festivals—Passover, Pentecost and (on the eighth day) Tabernacles. Prayers are offered for the repose of the departed ones' souls. Each person prays independently. In memory of a departed father, the prayer is offered in these words:

"May God remember the soul of my honored father [naming him], who has gone to his eternal home; on whose behalf I vow alms; by way of reward, be his soul bound up in the bundle of life with the souls of Abraham, Isaac and Jacob, Sarah, Rebecca, Rachel and Leah, and all other righteous men and women that are in the Garden of Eden; and let us say Amen." [6]

However impressive the entire service may be, its most significant feature is the imitation of the Temple service. In the liturgy for the afternoon, the *Avodah*, all the details of the ancient ceremonial are rehearsed with accuracy and evident pleasure. The cantor and his whole train of coadjutors call on their every power to render the liturgy in a way to stir the emotions of the worshipers. These quotations are typical of the first part of the ceremonial:

"Happy the eyes that saw the high-priest in his sacred vestment as he stood, clad in snow-white robes of purity and honor; as he poured forth the sevenfold sprinkling of the atoning blood.

Footnote: 5. From *Prayers for the Day of Atonement*.

Footnote: 6. From *Daily Prayer Book*, by Singer.

"Happy the eyes that saw the chief of the sons of Aaron holding up his hands in blessing, like the proud cedar of Lebanon compassed by palm trees round about. He was as the morning star risen out of the dark night, and as the sun casting his splendor upon the temple of the Most High; like a golden censer spreading rich perfume near and far, and as the cypress tree which reached high up toward the sky.

"Happy the ears that heard the thousand-voiced song of the Levites accompanying the sounds of the trumpets; the many-stringed harp and flute, in sweet and soul-stirring melodies echoing the praise of the Most High.

After a time a plaintive note is heard:

"Happy the eye that beheld all these, for verily to hear only of them afflicts our soul!

"Happy the eye that saw our Temple, and the joy ful assembly of our congregation; for verily to hear only of them afflicts our soul!

"But the iniquities of our fathers have caused the desolation of the Temple, and our sins have prolonged the period of our captivity!

"O may the rehearsal of these things procure forgiveness for us, and the affliction of our soul be the means of our pardon!" [7]

These prayers concluded, there begins *Minchah,* the prayer following *Musaf.* This is repeated by anyone in the congregation, without being chanted. Meanwhile the cantor and his assistants take a rest in preparation for their next task. This is the singing of *Neilah,* Conclusion or "The Closing of the Gates." Here the cantor's intercession for the congregation is expressed with more earnestness than had been evident before;

Footnote: 7. From *Prayers for the Day of Atonement.*

the prosperity and well-being of every one in the whole congregation during all the ensuing year depends entirely upon this last intercessory prayer. Therefore the cry:

"Open unto us, O God, the gates of mercy,
Before the closing of the gates,
Ere the day is done.
The day vanishes,
The sun is setting—
Let us enter Thy gates!"

The services close with recitation of the *Shema*. First, the reader and the congregation say these eleven words once: "Hear O Israel: The Lord our God, the Lord is one." Then follows a sentence given three times: "Blessed be his name, whose glorious Kingdom is forever and ever," and: "The Lord, He is God," repeated seven times.

A blast from the *Shofar* is the signal for every man to return to his inheritance—in hope that God has written his name in the book of Life. But it is only hope; there is no assurance in Rabbinical Judaism. The following, from the Talmud, is very characteristic of this uncertainty:

"When Rabbi Yochanan ben Zachi was sick unto death, his disciples came to visit him; and when he saw them he wept. Upon which his disciples exclaimed: 'Light of Israel! Pillar of the right! Mighty hammer! Why weepest thou?' He replied: 'If I were going to be led into the presence of a king, who is but flesh and blood, today here and tomorrow in the grave, whose anger could not endure forever and whom perhaps I might pacify with words, or bribe with money, yet with all that, I should weep. But now that I am about to enter the presence of the King of Kings, the Holy One—

54

blessed be He forever and ever!—whose anger would be everlasting, who is not to be pacified with words or bribed with money, and in whose presence there are two roads before me, one leading to Paradise and other into Hell, should I not weep?' " [8]

In complete contrast to the want of certainty of reconciliation with God that is evident in Judaism's observance of the Day of Atonement, Christianity offers to every one a blessed assurance. Our Hope is the Lord Jesus Christ Himself (I TIMOTHY 1:1). In Him there is for every soul, Gentile and also Jew:

1. Redemption through the blood of Christ (I PETER 1:18, 19).
2. Forgiveness through the blood (EPHESIANS 1:7).
3. Justification through the blood (ROMANS 5:9).
4. Peace through the blood (COLOSSIANS 1:20).
5. Sanctification through the blood (HEBREWS 13:12).
6. Victory through the blood (REVELATION 12:11).
7. Everlasting glory through the blood (REVELATION 7:14, 15).

Footnote: 8. *Berachoth,* fol. 28.

VII
THE FEAST OF TABERNACLES
Succoth

At a very early hour on the morrow after the Atonement Day, the religious Jew is once more on his way to the synagogue. His purpose is to show that his love for God is just as strong to-day as it was during the "fearful days" when he besought favors for the coming year. From the synagogue, having participated in the usual week-day prayers, he returns home to begin work on his *succah*.

The *succah* or booth is a structure especially built for the Feast of Tabernacles, or Booths. The booth is so thatched as to be a protection against the sun while yet allowing the stars to shine at night. It serves as a permanent dwelling during the seven days of the feast. All the males are required to live in it, unless prevented by ill health. In southern climates the *succah* is of such size as to enable the whole family to live in it during the seven days.

In LEVITICUS 23:42, 43 we read: "Ye shall dwell in booths seven days; all that are Israelites born shall dwell in booths; that your generations may know that I made the children of Israel to dwell in booths, when I brought them out of the land of Egypt." This passage, then, sets forth the historical significance of the feast and the aspect of it which is embodied in the name, *Chag-ha-Succoth*. This feast begins on the fifteenth of Tishri, five days after the Day of Atonement.

Chag-ha-Asif, the Feast of Ingatherings, is another name of the festival. This phrase reminds the Israelites of blessings gathered from the field. In recognition of this source of material benefits they are commanded to take *lulav,* a branch of the palm tree; *ethrog,* citron; *hadassim,* myrtle sprigs; and *araboth,* willows of the brook. They are to bind the willows together for convenience in lifting them up during the recitation of the *Hallel* (PSALMS 113-118), in the morning prayer.

Holding the *lulav* in his right hand, and the *ethrog* in his left, the worshiper recites the following blessing:

1. "Blessed art Thou, O Lord our God, King of the Universe, who hast sanctified us with Thy Commandments, and commanded us to take up the *Lulav.*"

2. "Blessed art Thou, O Lord our God, King of the Universe, who hast preserved us alive, sustained us and brought us to enjoy this season." [1]

At the close of the morning service the Torah (scroll of the Law) is taken from the Ark to the reading table (*bima*). A procession is formed, and the worshipers, prayer shawls over their heads and citrons and palm branches in their hands, make a circuit of the synagogue while this remarkable prayer is offered:

"For Thy sake, O our God, save now (Hosanna)!"

"For Thy sake, O our Creator, save now!"

"For Thy sake, O our Redeemer, save now!"

"For Thy Sake, O Thou who seekest for us, save now!" [2]

On the Sabbath day there is no such procession nor is use made of citron or palm branch. Carrying these articles to the synagogue would be a violation of one of the Sabbatic laws; it is regarded as a form of work.

Footnote: 1. From *Prayers for the Feast of Tabernacles.*

Footnote: 2. From *Prayers for the Feast of Tabernacles.*

The last day of the Feast of Succoth is called *Hoshana Rabba,* because on this day numerous petitions for the salvation of Israel are recited. There is a widespread belief among the Jews that the destinies which were pronounced and recorded in heaven at the Feast of the New Year, and sealed on the Day of Atonement, are being distributed on *Hoshana Rabba.* On this day, not merely one scroll (Torah) but all the scrolls found in the Ark are used for the processions round the synagogue, and a larger number of willows than usual is in the hands of every praying Jew; the last day's processions number seven.

At the completion of the procession the worshipers, now again in their places, begin the prayer: "Save, we beseech Thee Save Us, O God, for Thy Name's sake." Then, while uttering a petition for forgiveness of sins, each person shakes the bundle of willows or strikes it against the desk before him, till its leaves fall off. The Jews have a belief that for the leaves to come off quickly is a good sign; it indicates that the sins are forgiven. Each Jew, therefore, sees to it that the leaves of *Hoshana* (willow twigs tied together) are quickly fallen, even if he must strike them hard.

On the evening of this day, the "eighth day" commences (NUMBERS 29:35), at the same hour that the Sabbath begins. The orthodox Jew goes to the synagogue, for the evening service by which the Feast of *Shemini Atzereth* or eight-day festival is ushered in. On his return home the master of the family says *Kiddush,* the blessing over the cup of wine, as on the first night of the Feast of Tabernacles, but using the words, "This eight-day, the Feast of Solemn Assembly, the time of our rejoicing," because this festival is distinct from the Feast of Tabernacles.

The prayers for the day consist of *Hallel* (PSALMS 113-118), which is recited in full and the Book of Ecclesiastes is read, from a scroll.

A significant feature of the Feast of Tabernacles itself is its closing ceremonial, the Feast of *Simchot Torah*, "the rejoicing of the Law." It is so called because, the reading of the Pentateuch having been completed on this day, it is now the Jew's high privilege to begin reading it again. All the scrolls are taken out of the Ark. A procession is formed, headed by the reader. He is followed by men reverently carrying the scrolls. While they pass slowly around the synagogue they all sing:

"We beseech Thee, O Lord, save now!"

"We beseech Thee, O Lord, give success now!"

"We beseech Thee, O Lord, answer us when we call!" [3]

The procession continues until all the men present have taken part in it. After it is ended all the scrolls, except two are returned to the Ark, and the regular reading of the lesson commences. Every individual in the synagogue is called up to pronounce the blessing. The portion for this occasion extends from the 33rd chapter of Deuteronomy to the end of the book, and includes also the first chapter of Genesis. The Deuteronomy section is read over and over again, three verses for every person. No one may be omitted; not even children are exempt. If necessary, fathers carry smaller children forward, and pronounce the blessing for them. The person who reads the last section of Deuteronomy is called *Chathan Torah*, Bridegroom of the Law, and the one who reads from Genesis is called *Chathan Bereshith*, Bridegroom of Genesis.

Footnote: 3. From *Prayers for the Feast of Tabernacles.*

Simchot Torah is the only day in the year on which men and women, young and old, publicly rejoice over the Law. Their rejoicing reminds one of a certain joyful promise of Scripture, a promise which is yet to be fulfilled. Indeed, the real meaning of "the rejoicing of the Law" seems to lie just here; the feast is a type of the everlasting rest and never-ending joy foretold in JEREMIAH 31:31-34:

"Behold, the days come, saith the Lord, that I will make a new covenant with the house of Israel, and with the house of Judah: not according to the covenant that I made with their fathers in the day that I took them by the hand to bring them out of the land of Egypt; which my covenant they brake, although I was an husband unto them, saith the Lord.... I will put my law in their inward parts, and write it in their hearts; and will be their God, and they shall be my people. And they shall teach no more every man his neighbor, and every man his brother, saying, Know the Lord, for they shall all know me, from the least of them unto the greatest of them, saith the Lord: for I will forgive their iniquity, and I will remember their sin no more."

At that time, "the redeemed of Israel, having quitted their earthly tabernacles, as frail and fading as the arbours in which of old they dwelt during this festival, shall be received into the house not made with hands, the heavenly Temple; and as 'a great multitude which no man could number, of all nations, and kindreds, and people, and tongues,' shall stand 'before the throne, and before the lamb, clothed with white robes, and palms in their hands,' crying 'with a loud voice, saying, Salvation to our God, which sitteth upon the throne, and unto the lamb' (REVELATION 7:9-10)" [4]

Footnote: 4. From *"Moriah"* by Rev. Robert W. Fraser.

VIII
THE FEAST OF DEDICATION 36η
Hanukah

Most brilliant of all pages of Jewish history is that
which records the deeds of the Maccabean patriots and
martyrs. But it is a page deliberately torn from the
records of ancient Israel, for Talmudic Judaism disdains
to mention the exploits of the Maccabees. As some one
well remarked, "Jacob, whom Judas the Maccabee delivered, would have forgotten him had not the Christian
Church preserved the book."

One glorious fact, however, that not even Talmudic
Judaism could obliterate, is that commemorated by
Hanukah, the Feast of Dedication. This feast is asso-
ciated with an historical anniversary not mentioned in
the Bible, like *Purim* it is a minor festival, and it is not
invested with the same sacredness as the festivals commanded in the Torah. It calls Israel's memory back to
the victories of the Maccabees over Antiochus Epiphanes
in 160 B. C., that tyrant who was responsible for the
introduction of the Greek religious practices that were
an abomination to the Jews.

Greek thought and life must be honored for having
brought to the world the choicest fruits of logic, philosophy and art. The Greeks taught the esthetics of the
physical; lines, curves, form, light, and shadow they
understood perfectly. But the Jews gave the world
something better, for what they gave was not physical
but spiritual. They taught the world religion, the beauty

of righteousness, the lesson of the one God, the one universe, the one humanity. Israel's prophets derided injustice, declaimed against man's inhumanity to man. They were enemies of the oppressor. They pleaded in behalf of the stranger, the widow, the orphan. They challenged kings and princes, showed the futility of armaments for war. Their pictures were painted not on canvas but on the hearts of men. They dreamed dreams of universal peace. They anticipated all the social legislation and reform of the present century. With the Word of God, as their textbook, they taught the way for other faiths.

It was to preserve all this that Judas Maccabeus and his heroic little band, inspired by the aged Mattathias, defied a mighty nation, rescued the Temple, and saved the faith from pollution. —

That final victory of the Maccabean armies over all the hosts of Syria was won, according to the Hebrew calendar, "on the five and twentieth day of the month called Kislev [in December]. There was great gladness among the people as they offered sacrifices according to the law on the new altar, praising God because the reproach of the heathen was put away. Moreover, Judas and his brethren, with the whole congregation of Israel, ordained that the days of the dedication of the altar be kept in their season from year to year, by the space of eight days from the five and twentieth day of the month of Kislev." [1]

This feast is also called the Feast of Lights, because of the miracle recorded in connection with the rededication of the Temple. The Talmud tells us that when the Jews had overpowered their enemies and re-entered the Temple, the priests desired to light the lamp which

---

Footnote: 1. From *The Book of the Maccabees.*

was to burn continually before the Lord (EXODUS 27:20, 21); they found a bottle of pure oil, enough to last for only one day. But a miracle happened; it lasted eight days. To recall God's mercies, and to "publish His power to perform miracles," the Jew to this day celebrates this feast by the kindling of lights on every evening of the festival. On the eve of the first day one light is kindled; on the second two, and so up to eight on the eve of the eighth day. The *Hanukah* lamp is set near a window, so that people passing may see it and thus learn of the graciousness and power of God. At the lighting of the candles, or oil lamps, the following benedictions are said:

"Blessed art Thou, O Lord our God, King of the universe, who hast sanctified us by Thy commandments and commanded us to kindle the light of *Hanukah*.

Blessed art Thou, O Lord our God, King of the universe, who didst work miracles for our fathers, in those days at this season." [2]

A long hymn is sung after the benedictions and while the candles are burning. The lights must burn for at least thirty minutes, during which time no work of any kind may be done; the period is spent in play and merriment.

During this feast the prayers are the regular week-day prayers, with only one addition—that of *al-Hanisim*, enumerating the victories celebrated by the occasion. A few of the usual short prayers like Psalms 6 and 20 are omitted, but instead the great song of praise, *Hallel*, PSALMS 113-118, is sung daily, and several verses of NUMBERS 7 are read each day. On the Sabbath day during the week of *Hanukah* the lesson from the prophets is taken from ZECHARIAH 2:4-7.

Footnote: 2. *Shulchan Aruch*, 139.

Dr. Cassell, a Hebrew scholar, believes that Christmas with its December 25th date, carries us back not to a festival of heathen origin, as some would have us think, but to the Jewish Feast of Dedication. He points out that the heathen always refused to accept anything of Christian origin, and that the customs of Christmas are significantly in accord with those of the Dedication festival.

There exists a still more stable basis for connecting Jewish feast and Christian festival, however. It is found both in the aspect of dedication and in that of light. Christ is the true Temple, and His incarnation is the real Temple dedication. Moreover, out from Him has shined "a Light to lighten the Gentiles, and the glory of thy people Israel." It is for us who walk in His light to use every effort to lead Israel to rejoice not in any flickering lights of a man-made origin, but in the steadfast eternal radiance of the glory of God in Jesus Christ. Under the power of the Spirit, let every Jew learn to know Him who is "the true Light," the Light of the World. "O house of Jacob, come ye, and let us walk in the light of the Lord" (ISAIAH 2:5).

IX
THE FEAST OF LOTS
Purim

Esther's feast is celebrated on the thirteenth of Adar (the second Adar, in leap year). The evening of that day and the whole of the day following constitute the Feast of *Purim,* commemorating the events related so graphically in the *megillah,* or scroll containing the story of the book of Esther. *"Purim,"* an old Persian word, means "lots," and the day is so called after the lots cast by Haman to determine a favorable time for carrying out his evil intentions.

The method of celebrating *Purim* is characteristic. The feast finds its expression in terms of social service. Generosity and joy abound. Whatever may be the self-denials of the year, this feast is the time of outflow. There is much sending of gifts to the poor, *shalach Monos,* as well as to friends. "Merry Purim!" "Happy Purim!" are the greetings exchanged, and in fact it is a "merry Purim" only when it has been made a really "happy Purim" for the family and for others.

At the synagogue the evening service is attended by young and old, the old to read the *Megillah* and the young to "beat old Haman once more." This is the one time in the year when a Jewish youngster may make all the noise he wishes to. When the reader of the scroll comes to the name of Haman it is his "inalienable right" to stamp with his feet, strike the benches, and shout: *"Ymach shemo!"* (let his name be blotted out), or *"Arur Haman!"* (cursed be Haman). But when the name of

Mordecai or of Esther is mentioned, the cry joyfully changes to: *"Baruch Mordecai!" "Baruch Esther!"* (blessed be Mordecai, blessed be Esther).

Jews of the past placed themselves on record as firm believers in the Old Testament Scriptures by observing this feast and other festivals year after year since they were instituted. The Book narrating the facts which these festivals commemorate is in our own hands; the Jew himself is the best proof that the Bible is true. And those ancient Scriptures, so authenticated by Israel, testify of a Saviour greater than Esther, greater than Mordecai—Jesus, Messiah of Israel.

X

MINOR FESTIVALS AND FASTS

Several occasions during the Jewish year call for mention in addition to the feasts and fasts already enumerated. First, two which have some relation to nature and the seasons:

1. *Rosh Chodesh,* New Moon Day. Originally this was regarded as a solemn occasion. In the course of time, however, it lost much of its significance. Orthodox Jews observe it by the chanting of the Hallel (PSALMS 113-118), and by the reading of a portion of the Pentateuch (NUMBERS 28:11-15), which refers to the sacrifices of this day.

2. *Chamishoh Osor Be-Shevat,* the fifteenth day of Shevat (February), is the Jewish Arbor Day or "the New Year of the Trees." On that day it is customary to eat a great variety of fruits. A special fruit for the day seems to be "St. John's Bread." In Palestine, school children use the day each year for planting many trees.

In commemoration of sad events in our history, chiefly occurrences connected with the fall of Jerusalem, a number of fast days were instituted:

1. *Assoroh Beteves,* the tenth of Teves, recalls the day when Nebuchadnezzar began the siege of Jerusalem.

2. *Shivo-Osor be-Tammuz,* the seventeenth of Tammuz, is the day when Nebuchadnezzar entered the city through a breach. Later Titus also entered the Holy City on this day.

3. *Tisha B'av,* the ninth of Av, commemorates the destruction of the first Temple by the Babylonians and

the last by the Romans). (see Chapter IV, on "Tisha B'av," in this book).

4. *Tzom Gedaliah,* the Fast of Gedaliah, falls on the third of Tishri and commemorates the assassination of the governor Gedaliah of the house of David, whom Nebuchadnezzar placed in authority in Palestine after the downfall of Jerusalem. This event marked the climax in the disasters that befell the first Jewish Commonwealth.

5. *Taanith Esther,* the Fast of Esther, is observed on the thirteenth of Adar, in commemoration of Esther's fast recorded in the Bible (see Chapter IX, "The Feast of Lots").

XI
THE DAY OF REST
Shabbes

Observance of the Sabbath was sanctioned by the highest of all authorities. Its establishment is coeval with the earliest intimations of the divine will, and of the first promises of divine mercy and love to man. Later the institution formed part of the moral law, becoming a part of the Ten Commandments.

But it is to be noticed that the observance of the Sabbath, as commanded in the Bible, consisted merely in refraining from labor. We read of no other Sabbath laws than such as are found in EXODUS 20:8-11:

"Remember the sabbath day, to keep it holy. Six days shalt thou labor, and do all thy work: but the seventh day is the sabbath of the Lord thy God: in it thou shalt not do any work, thou, nor thy son, nor thy daughter, thy manservant, nor thy maidservant, nor thy cattle, nor thy stranger that is within thy gates: for in six days the Lord made heaven and earth, the sea, and all that in them is, and rested the seventh day: wherefore the Lord blessed the sabbath day, and hallowed it."

To this simple requirement our Rabbis, little by little, added command upon command, and precept upon precept, until at length the Sabbath became a burden too heavy to be borne.

Of those innumerable laws relating to the Sabbath only a few can be here enumerated. Jewish women, maid-servants and girls, for example, are warned not to order a Gentile woman on the Sabbath to do this or that, but they are permitted to instruct her on a week day what she is to do on the Sabbath.

Radishes are not to be salted in quantities. Each piece is to be dipped separately in salt while it is being eaten.

A Jew should be very careful of any fur garment he may be wearing, lest unwittingly he pluck a hair therefrom. For the same reason he is not to rub his head or touch his beard on the Sabbath. He is not to wash his hands with either soap or salt on the Sabbath, nor on that day may he play ball.

No geese, fowls, cats or dogs are to be handled on the Sabbath.

Let no pocket handkerchiefs or spectacles be carried on the Sabbath in any unwalled city.

It is a sin to lift a stone, or even money, on the Sabbath day. But here the Rabbis make a noteworthy distinction: "A man may lift up his son, even though he [the child] has a stone in his hand. If money be on a cushion, he may transfer the money by shaking the cushion." [1] In this connection I recall a striking incident from my own life.

As a youth, while with my father on the way to the synagogue one Sabbath morning, I was attracted by a few pieces of silver money scattered on the ground. Both Father and I looked; neither one of us knew exactly what to do. I must confess that had I been alone on that beautiful Sabbath morning I would have settled the matter right there and then, and in my pocket there would have jingled some silver coins as I proceeded to the Synagogue. After a few moments' hesitation my father recalled a Rabbinical bit of advice. [2] With his foot he

Footnote: 1. *Kitzur Sh'lh,* fols. 65-67.

Footnote: 2. *Shabbath,* Fol. 153, col. 1.

shoved the money into a corner and covered it with sand, hoping that in the evening he could return, and find it there. We did go back after the Sabbath day, but to our sorrow the money was gone. Some Jew had broken the Sabbath.

There was all too much foundation for our Lord's charge that the Pharisees had laid on men's shoulders too grievous burdens. The ceremonial law itself was a burden which, as the apostles later declared, neither they nor their fathers were able to carry. It was therefore the duty of the interpreters of the Law to lighten its pressure by wise and right interpretations, instead of increasing its severity. They had, as a matter of history, rendered it an intolerable burden. They had transformed the Sabbath of the Lord into an object of idolatrous homage—as if "man were made for the Sabbath." From their disregard of human rights and divine mercy the orthodox Jew still suffers.

Here, then, is a picture of the Sabbath as kept today among the very few Jews who still follow the teachings of the Rabbis.

On Friday morning preparations start. These include, besides the cooking of the regular meals and special Sabbath dishes, such as filled fish, *lokshen* and *tzimmes,* the provision of special table appointments; that is, the Sabbath lights, the loaves of Sabbath bread and the wine for *Kiddush.*

In the evening, before sunset, the wife lights the candles, repeating as she does so the following benediction, which every woman must know whether literate or not:

"Blessed art Thou, O Lord our God, King of the universe, who hast sanctified us by Thy Commandments, and commanded us to kindle the Sabbath lights."

For the men the services begin at the synagogue, where the daily prayers (*Mincha*) are read, after which some special Psalms are recited and a hymn, *Lecha Dodi*, is sung. These are the words of *Lecha Dodi*:

Come forth, my friend, the bride to meet;
Come O my friend, the Sabbath greet!
"Observe ye" and "remember" still
The Sabbath—thus His holy will
God in one utterance did proclaim.
The Lord is one, and one His Name—
To His renown and praise and fame.
      Come forth, etc.

Greet we the Sabbath at our door,
Wellspring of blessing evermore,
With everlasting gladness fraught;
Of old ordained, divinely taught,
Last in creation, first in thought.
      Come forth, etc.

Arouse thyself, awake and shine,
For lo! it comes, the light divine.
Give forth a song, for over thee
The glory of the Lord shall be
Revealed in beauty speedily.
      Come forth, etc.

Crown of thy husband, come in peace,
Come, bidding toil and trouble cease.
With joy and cheerfulness abide
Among thy people true and tried,
Thy faithful people—come, O bride!
      Come forth, my friend, the bride to meet,
      Come, O my friend, the Sabbath greet! [3]

When the father of the house returns home from

Footnote: 3. *Singer*; page 111, translated by Mrs. H .Lucas.

the synagogue he blesses his wife and children. Then
the male members of the family unite in singing *Shalom
Alechem*, a hymn built on a statement in the Talmud to
the effect that two angels accompany each man from the
synagogue on Sabbath eve, and remain with the household during the Sabbath day. The father recites PRO-
VERBS 31:10-31, complimenting his wife on her part in
bringing in the Sabbath joy, make *Kiddush* over a glass
of wine, and then begins to partake of the Sabbath feast.

In the morning the Jew is again on the way to the
synagogue. There, with others, he prays the morning
prayer, *Shachrith*, and listens to the reading of the
weekly portion of the Torah, and Haftorah, a portion
from the prophets.

Three services are held during the day. On the
father's return from the last, called *Maariv*, a wax candle
is lighted, and over a glass of wine he chants the *Hab-
dalah* (separation) benediction; that is, the "separation"
between the Sabbath and the week days, between the
sacred and the profane.

The Rabbis promised: "Whosoever keeps the Sabbath according to its constitution, even though he were
an idolater like Enosh, he shall be forgiven." As a matter of fact, this is not Scriptural. Keeping Sabbaths
was never a means of obtaining forgiveness from God.
EXODUS 31:16, 17 shows God's purpose in giving the
day. "It is a sign" or seal of His covenant with His
people; its Sabbath rest is an emblem of the peace which
passeth all understanding, given to the people whom
God hath delivered both from Egypt and from spiritual
bondage.

XII
VOICES OF THE GHETTO

For centuries Israel has been kept together in the bonds of Rabbinical law. Locked within the walls of Ghetto, surrounded on every hand by oppressors, the Jew found joy, consolation and release from all that tended to make him the most miserable member of the human family, by the return of each feast. During the festival he and his relived the joyous experiences of his fathers as he, in spirit, walked with them through the sacred places so dear to his heart.

But that was the experience of the Jew within the Ghetto walls. Today the gates are open, the Ghetto walls are crumbling. Many of Israel's sons and daughters are now in open revolt against the synagogue and all of its inhibitions. [1]

A widespread belief is found among the Gentiles, and even among many Christians, that of all religious denominations Judaism alone offers an ideal unity of doctrine, one which all Jews share. This is a great mistake. The cause of the error lies in the fact that they are acquainted with only one kind of Judaism—the Judaism of fiction. The Judaism described in books and magazines generally has in mind "our neighbors the Gentiles," and is therefore very beautiful to the eye. As one Jewish writer puts it: "It is the Judaism of three dimensions: length, breadth and thickness, with emphasis on thickness. It finds its greatest expression in size, in externals;

Footnote:1. *American Judaism,* by Joseph Lesser.

74

and howsoever empty it may be from within, it looks imposing from without." [2]

But there is another and real Judaism, one that is altogether different. It is the Judaism of which we Jewish Christians have been a part—the Judaism of the Ghetto. With this Judaism I want the readers of this chapter to become acquainted.

Once there was a time, in Israel's long exile, when only one voice was heard throughout the camp. It was the voice of God calling young and old to follow Him. But now many are the voices which call the children of the Ghetto. They urge the Jews to become followers of very diverse "isms," each voice assuring them that its way is the only "right way."

There is the voice of Orthodoxy. All adherents of Orthodox Judaism are asked to accept as their creed the "Thirteen Articles" of faith which the great Jewish philosopher, Maimonides, formulated at the close of the twelfth century. These articles teach God's existence, unity, incorporeality and eternity. They acknowledge that He is the sole object of man's worship; that prophecy is true; that Moses is the supreme authority, and that the Law which he committed to Israel is of divine origin and immutable; that a divine judgment and retribution is to come; that the Messiah is to appear; and that the dead shall be raised again.

But when Orthodox Judaism acknowledges the divine origin and immutability of the Law of Moses, it adds: "Both written and oral Law." This one phrase puts the Rabbinical writings on an equality with the Word of God. It demands of its adherents that their lives be regulated according to the teachings of men. Orthodox Judaism is, to quote a Jewish writer, "the

Footnote: 2. *The Reflex*, by Dr. Max Raisin.

type of Judaism that expresses itself in a hat, a hank of hair for a beard, a kosher sign on a butcher shop, and a prayer book in Hebrew which the people do not understand."

How is this voice received in the Ghetto of today? For a convincing answer visit any one of the synagogues in a Jewish neighborhood during the hours of prayer. But be sure not to visit it on the New Year or the Day of Atonement. These are the two days when the synagogues are crowded. At any other time during the year our orthodox brethren struggle to gather a quorum— the Rabbinical number of ten men required for public prayer. The synagogues are empty, save for two or three old men brought over by their children from Russia or Galacia, who come to the *Beth-Hamidrash,* either to look into a *Perek Mishnaees* (Talmudical treatise) or to escape the "talks" of their Jewish daughters-in-law.

A second voice in the Ghetto is that of Reform Judaism. The Reform movement had its origin in Germany with Moses Mendelssohn. Reform Jews have thoroughly sifted Rabbinical Judaism. They have discovered so many exceptions, alleviations and mitigations, and introduced so many reforms, that their's is an altogether new Judaism, in life and practice as well as in public worship.

But it is not only the binding authority of the Talmud that they have discarded. In a measure they have also abandoned the divine origin and binding authority of Moses and the prophets. It is neither the Bible nor the Talmud that Reform Jews follow. They have selected from the Old Testament and the Talmud that which best suits their rationalistic mind, and which seems to them compatible with modern thought and life. Reform Judaism rejects the Bible as God's holy word, and asserts that a personal Messiah was never promised; the prophecy was only of a Messianic Age. It does not believe in a bodily resurrection of the dead. As late as 1869, the Central Conference of American Rabbis resolved that: "The belief in the resurrection of the body has no religious foundation in Judaism, and the doctrine of immortality refers to the after existence of the soul only." [3]

Is this voice more successful than the voice of Orthodoxy? Here is the answer, given by one of their own number. Rabbi I. Newman, formerly of the Reformed Temple Emmanu El, San Francisco, while speaking to a class of graduating Rabbis said: "Liberal Judaism is a faith for the few, and not for the many. It is more an adaptation to economic and political circumstances than a unique spiritual revelation. It is motivated more by fear than by prophecy. It has sought to overcome fundamentalism, avoid sensationalism, and outdistance modernism. But it has studiously sidestepped the major issues of the present-day life." Reform Judaism as expounded by its preachers is literary, ethical and cultured. But it lacks prophetic vision.

Another Rabbi, writing on the subject of the Jewish youth, says that the reason of Jewish young people's indifference to the Jewish religion is that "they hail either from homes which are presumed to be orthodox but which in fact are exponents of a kind of religion which is of the Ghetto type and which is not always impressive, or from so-called 'reformed' Jewish homes, which means that Judaism had long ago ceased to be observed as a real and vital part of the lives of the people. They attended temples where the Rabbis spoke on everything but religion, where novels and motion picture were

Footnote: 3. Platform of Pittsburgh Conference, Article VII.

made the themes of sermons rather than the lessons to be gotten from God's Holy Word." [4] Reform Judaism obviously has nothing for the longing Jewish soul.

A third voice heard in the Ghetto of today is that of Zionism. "And Zionism," one is accustomed to hear, "is merely the awakening of the Jewish national soul under the pressure of persecution and antisemitism. It is not in any sense the working of a deep religious impulse." But this is contrary to historical facts. Long before the day of Dr. Theodore Herzel, the father of Political Zionism, there was a deep longing in the heart of the Ghetto Jew for the land of his fathers. No other people in history has identified itself in joy and sorrow—and always in aspiration—with a single land so completely, and that a land known to us only in prayer, in idea and in vision. Israel's prayers for centuries have been:

"Rebuild Jerusalem speedily in our days as an everlasting building." [5]

"Bring us with exultation to Zion, Thy City, and to Jerusalem, Thy Sanctuary, with everlasting joy." [6]

Such were the prayers and aspirations of the Zionists of the past, but the modern Zionists, comprising Jews from every walk of life, differ greatly. The late well-known Jacob Schiff based his objections to modern Zionism on the ground that "from fifty to seventy-five per cent. of the so-called Jewish Nationalists are either atheists or agnostics, and that the great majority of its leaders have absolutely no interest in the Jewish religion." Such Zionist leaders of the past and present as Dr. Herzl, Max Nordau, Israel Zangwill, Dr. Weitz-

---

Footnote: 4. Rabbi Magnin, in *B'nai B'rith Magazine.*

Footnote: 5. *Prayer for the Afternoon.*

Footnote: 6. *Prayer for the New Moon.*

mann, Nahum Sokolow, Lewis Lipsky, Vladimir Jabotinsky and many others voiced not the prophetic summons: "Come, let us go up to the mountain of Jehovah," but "Let us go to Palestine, the land of our fathers, that we also may be like all the nations."

Still another prominent voice in the modern Ghetto, a voice that attracts a great number of Jews, is that of Radicalism. It is vain to hide the fact. It is undeniable that the Jew has been conspicuous in the modern radical movements of the world. In America the radical forums of our larger cities are largely attended by descendants of Abraham, Isaac and Jacob. The Jewish worker and the intellectual of the Ghetto live in a world of lectures, debates, dreams and hopes that teem with the newest ideas of social change. Two of the leading Jewish newspapers in this country, *Forward* and *Freiheit*, are the official publications of radical groups. Trades unions like the Amalgamated Clothing Workers and The International Garment Workers of America are intensely radical in their immediate as well as ultimate aims. Radicalism is almost a religion to the one that enters its folds.

There are a multitude of other voices in the Ghetto. Among these reference is due to Christian Science. This teaching is taking thousands from Israel's fold. Spiritualism, Catholicism and even Theosophy have also made serious inroads into modern Jewry.

In the midst of this Babel of voices there is also the still small Voice of God, speaking through the Jewish Missionary. He pleads with men and women, young and old, to repent of their sins and to accept Him who came to "save his people."

79

XIII

THE VOICE OF GOD

God is speaking in the Ghetto. Does the Ghetto hear? It is the universal conviction of students of contemporary Jewish life that never has there been such a manifest interest in the Christian faith among Jews as is evident today. Is it not for the Christian to determine whether that remarkable interest is to bear its intended fruit in the Salvation of Israel?

Certain truths of deep concern to both Jews and Christians seem to be suggested by the foregoing chapters. Among the significant facts which have been outlined the following appear to be outstanding:

1. *Christianity is a direct development of Jewish history and life.* Israel and the Church are inseparable. What Israel Zangwill said to his own people holds true for Christians as well: "We shall never get the future straight until we disentangle the past."

2. *The Christian is debtor to the Jew.* It was the Jew who preserved for us the oracles of God, through long periods of darkness, danger and corruption. His feasts and fasts of today turn his thoughts to the very Scriptures that form the genesis of our Christian faith.

3. *Many Jewish customs are symbolic of Christian truths.* The close relationship between the Passover and the Lord's Supper, for example, is obvious. The Feast of Dedication suggests not only Christmas, but the dedicating of life and service to Christ. But more significant than this, or than the historical connection between Pentecost and the Feast of Weeks, is the intimate bond

between the Jewish Day of Atonement and the Sacrifice on Calvary. Ignorant of the power of Calvary's blood to reconcile them to God, the religious-minded Jews cry aloud, hour after hour, and year after year through the centuries: "For the sin for which we have incurred the penalty of death from the hand of God....forgive us, pardon us, grant us atonement!"

4. *Sadness is typical of modern Jewish life.* Whatever the joyous feast or meditative fast, each religious occasion turns mind and soul of the Jew toward his two overmastering sorrows. The one is over his nation's vanished glories, the other grows out of his own want of assurance that his desperate prayers for pardon will ever be answered. He prays to the Father, but not to the Father's eternal Son.

5. *Jewry today is hungry for the Bread of Life.* Never in the history of my people has there been such a spiritual restlessness and hunger as just now. That hunger, unsatisfied by the ritual of synagogue and seasonal feasts, for all their deeply religious background, can find its satisfaction only in Him who said: "He that cometh to me shall never hunger."

6. *Spirituality characterizes the Jewish feasts and fasts.* As delivered by our forefathers, and as practiced today, Israel's ceremonial observances are essentially religious. Their basis is an invincible faith in God. He is theirs, and they are His. In all their thinking, in all their praying, they see Him who is invisible.

7. *To maintain the old ceremonies in all their spiritual purity becomes increasingly difficult.* Many of the older men and women of Israel are faithful, but new days and new ways are gravely threatening their influence. Large numbers of Israel's sons and daughters are in secret or open rebellion. They turn eager ears to

the "voices of the Ghetto," and to the one trustworthy Voice among these they pay the least heed.

8. *The Jew is in need of Christian sympathetic understanding.* If the needs of my people are regarded only from the consideration that Jews are fellow human beings, it is evident that they are in need of human sympathy and human understanding. They require that we have more than a reading of fiction giving a one-sided view of Ghetto life. Not a surface knowledge of minor externals but a genuine knowledge of daily life and daily thought, this is what the Jew's heart asks of his Christian neighbors.

9. *The Jew needs Christ.* Surely there can be no doubt of it. Do not his feasts and his fasts show his need of Christ? Practically every page of the preceding chapters reveals the fact that what the Jews seeks in them he can in reality find only in his Messiah.

He is capable of honoring and accepting Christ. As of old Jewish disciples received Him, so He is being accepted by numerous Jewish disciples today. Mary, his Jewish mother, believed in him, as did Peter the Jew, John the Jew, Paul the Jew, and all the host of His Jewish followers. In our own times, He is honored by numerous Jewish leaders. Israel Zangwill regarded the coming of Jesus to earth as "a burst of sunshine" on a darkened world. Rabbi Henry Berkovitz has found in Jesus "The very flowering of Judaism." Morris Jastrow once recorded his conviction that "the long hoped-for reconciliation between Judaism and Christianity will come when once the teachings of Jesus shall have become the axioms of human conduct."

The vision of these illustrious Jews was imperfect, they saw through a glass darkly, they were unable to open their eyes to the full glory of the Son of God. But in all ages there have been other Jews, equally distinguished and more blest, who have boldly fixed their gaze forever upon Christ; [1] and there are such Jews today. In almost every Ghetto one can find them, humble and happy disciples of Jesus, living earnest Christian lives, in many instances going about among their disconsolate brethren of the house of Israel, doing Christian deeds and offering Christian assurance of hope in Him who loved us all, and gave Himself for us all.

After His resurrection Christ spoke these words to my Jewish brethren of the first century: "Go ye.... and make disciples of all the nations." The Jewish apostles delivered that Great Commission to other Christians, and so it has come to us of today. Are we not justified in believing that this commission involves such privileges for every Christian as the following?

1. Cooperating in carrying the New Testament to the Jews.

2. Cooperating in preaching to the Jews the Gospel of Christ.

3. Cooperating with all Churches, Christian organizations and missionaries engaged in the task of enabling the Jews of our own day to reclaim that Messiah whom they rejected in the days when Jews first preached the Risen Christ.

In the light of eighteen years of experience as a Jewish missionary, it is my earnest conviction that we are now living in a day when great numbers of Jews can be brought into real fellowship with their rejected Messiah. Hundreds of men and women who in former years threw stones at the missionary, now stand for an hour or longer to listen to an open-air preacher of the Gospel. The

---

Footnote: 1. *See appendix III.*

very men who several years ago would not even allow a New Testament to touch their fingers or their garments, now willingly pay money for copies of this very book. Hundreds of Israel's intellectuals purchase Klausner's *Life of Jesus*, compare it with the New Testament, and devour anything and everything written regarding their long looked-for Messiah. Are these not infallible signs of Israel's spiritual need, and tokens of the timeliness of an energetic work of evangelism among the Jews?

God's word reveals two facts regarding Jewish evangelization which are too seldom remembered. The first is regarding God's love for His people Israel. To Israel He said: "I have loved thee with an everlasting love" (JEREMIAH 31:3), and also: "The mountains shall depart, and the hills be removed; but my kindness shall not depart from thee, neither shall the covenant of my peace" (ISAIAH 54:10). God's purpose is to redeem Israel. The second fact is regarding God's love for His children who minister to Israel. To a representative of Israel He said: "I will bless them that bless thee."

In the light of our heavenly Father's attitude toward Israel and toward us, and of the yearnings of Jews after Him, what shall we do for them?

"The Word of Life, if prized by you,
We owe to the despised Jew;
In all their wanderings, far and near,
His Word was sent their hearts to cheer;
Preserved by them, and handed down,
We see their light-their Savior own;
Then on your knees, before His throne,
  Remember oft the Jew."

"If Christ, the Lord, is prized by you,
He once was a despised Jew;
Without a spot to lay His head;
For you He came, and lived, and bled;
And can you then refuse to feel
Compassion for His nation's weal?
Their griefs might break a heart of steel-
  Oh pity then the Jew!"

"If we would 'prosper' all life through,
Still Zion's peace we must pursue;
Though trodden down, the Jews shall rise
And own that Christ they now despise;
Then lend your every aid to bring
The Alien Jew to Christ our King,
That Jew with Gentile soon may sing,
  'Salvation to the Lamb!'"

"We dare not, will not, hence refuse
To love, and feel, and pray for Jews.
O praise our God! Through Abraham's race
Came *Light*, and *Christ*, and *promised* grace
Then, God of Abraham, hear our cries
Remove the veil from Israel's eyes;
Make Jews and Gentiles truly wise,
  And Jesus all in all!"

APPENDIX I.
The Jewish Calendar

The months are luner, beginning with the new moon. The day is reckoned from evening to evening, and begins when three stars are visible, about twenty-five mintues after sunset.

The English word "month" is derived from the word "moon"; the Hebrew words for month are *yerach* (from yereach, the "moon") and *chodesh,* the moon's "renewal," *molad* or "birth." Its length should be about 29½ days. But as it would have been very inconvenient to divide a day between two months, the Jewish months alternately consist of 29 and 30 days. Twelve such months make a total of 354 days, while the solar year contains 365 days, therefore the extra month-the second Adar-to certain years which are called "leap years."

Before the Babylonian Exile the months had Jewish names and were usually indicated by numbers (*first month, second month, etc.*); but after the exile the Babylonian names were introduced, and are still in use among the Jews. These are:—

I.-NISAN.

Days:

1 New Moon.
14 The preparation of the Passover and the Paschal Sacrifice.
15 First Day of the Feast of Unleavened Bread.
16 Waving of the first-ripe Omer.
21 Close of the Passover.

II.-IYAR.

1 New Moon.

18 Lag-le-Omer, or the 33rd day in Omer.

III.-SIVAN.

1 New Moon.

6 Feast of Weeks; or Pentecost-seven weeks, or 50 days
after the beginning of the Passover,
when the two loaves of first-ripe wheat
were "waved," commemorative also of
the giving of the Law on Mount Sinai.

IV.-TAMMUZ.

1 New Moon.

17 Fast; taking of Jerusalem by Nebuchadnezzar.

V.-AV.

1 New Moon.

9 Fast; destruction of the Temple.

VI.-ELUL.

Days:

1 New Moon.

VII.-TISHRI.

1,-2 New Year's Feast.

3 Fast for the murder of Gedaliah.

10 Day of Atonement; Great Fast.

15 Feast of Tabernacles.

21 Close of Feast of Tabernacles.

22 Octave of the Feast of Tabernacles. In the Synagogues, on the 23rd. It is *Simchot Torah,* Feast
of the Annual Completion of the Reading of the Law.

VIII.-CHESHVAN.

1 New Moon.

IX.-CHISLEU.

1 New Moon.

25 Feast of the Dedication of the Temple-*Hanukah,*
lasting eight days.

X.-TEBETH.

 1 New Moon.
10 Fast on account of the Siege of Jerusalem.

XI.-SHEBAT.

 1 New Moon.

XII.-ADAR.

 1 New Moon.
13 Fast of Esther.
14 Purim, the Feast of Lots.

APPENDIX II.
The Talmud or Oral Law

The fundamental idea of the Talmud is that of Tradition. The word itself means "teaching," especially the teaching of the Law. The Talmud rests upon the belief, which has prevailed for centuries among the Jews, that on Mount Sinai in addition to the Written Law, another, the Oral Law was given from God to Moses. This Oral Law, which was to supplement or explain the Written Law, was supposed to have been repeated by Moses to Joshua, and by him to the elders of Israel, and then to have been handed down by them to their successors, and so on till the time of Ezra, when it became the possession of the "Men of the Great Synagogue." In this College of teachers there were such men as Haggai the Prophet (B.C. 520) and Simon the Just (B.C.300). From the time of the latter the Oral Law was handed down by a succession of learned men among whom was the great Rabbi Hillel, who lived at the time of our Lord. From the days of Hillel the traditional text of the Oral Law is supposed to have remained fixed and unaltered. He is said to have classified the whole of the Oral Law into six section called *Sedarim* into which the Talmud is divided. But it was Rabbi Jehudah Hannasi (A.D.191) who put them into writing.

There are two Talmuds, the Yerushalmi, or the Palestinian, and the Babli, that is, the Babylonian. The Talmud Yerushalmi gives the traditional saying of the Palestinian Rabbis; whereas the Talmud Babli gives the traditional sayings of the Rabbis of Babylon. This is by far the most popular among Talmudic students.

To the Orthodox Jew of the past, the Talmud was like the encircling ocean; it inserted itself into, and made itself felt in every nook and corner of the sphere of his existence. Like an atmosphere, it encompassed the whole round of his being, penetrated into all centers of vitality, and pressed with its incubent weight on every class irrespective of age, sex, or rank. It covered the whole field of life, and its principles affected every thought and every action of every member in the Jewish Ghetto.

The opinon of the modern Jew is very far from his brother of 18th or 19th century. The supernatural origin of the Talmud is rejected by him as superstition, and many parts of its teaching are at once set aside as idle tales. There are many lofty principles of morality and ethical doctrines to be admired, but to say, as some do, that the teachings of the Talmud are superior to those of the New Testament is certainly not true and far fetched.

APPENDIX III
A Few Eminent Hebrew Christians

ALEKAYEYEV, ALEXANDER (Distinguished Russian Writer).

ALEXANDER, RT. REV. M.S., D.D. (First Anglican Bishop of Jerusalem).

ASHER, BEN LEVI (fourth century).

AUGUST, J. J. (Lector of Oriental Languages at University of Laipzig).

BARON, DAVID (Author and Linguist).

BARTHOLODY, JACOB LEVI (Uncle of Felix Mendelssohn, and Officer in German Army).

BENDEMANN, EDWARD (Famous Painter).

BENEDICT, SIR H. (English Musician).

BERGER, REV. DAVID I. (Dean, Presb. Seminary, U. S.)

BERMAN, REV. P. L. (Presbyterian minister, U. S.)

BIRNBAUM, PROF. SOLOMON.

BRANISS, C. J. (Professor of Philosophy, Breslau, Germany).

BRAVIN, REV. DAN B. (Lutheran minister to the Jews, U. S.)

BRONSTEIN, REV. DAVID (Presbyterian minister and Director of Peniel Community Center in U. S.)

BUENA, FRANCISCO (Spanish Poet)

BURNHAM, LORD (Owner of Daily Telegraph, London).

CASSEL, REV. PAULUS, D.D. (Author and Court Preacher, Germany).

CENTZ, REV. H. B. (Presbyterian minister, in U. S.)

CHWOLSON, DANIEL ABRAMOVICH (Russian Orientalist, Famous Author).

COHN, REV. LEOPOLD, D. D. (Ex-Rabbi).

CONTRAT, MOSE (Professor of Roman Law at the University of Zurich and Amsterdam).

DA COSTA, DR. ISAAC (Dutch Historian and Poet).

DISRAELI, BENJAMIN, K. G. (Lord Beaconsfield).

EDERSHEIM, REV. ALFRED (Author "Life and Times of Jesus the Messiah," Oxford, England).

EINSPRUCH, REV. H. (Lutheran minister to the Jews and author of many valuable tracts).

EHRLICH, DAVID (Ex-Rabbi).

FLACKS, REV. JOSEPH (Presbyterian minister and Bible Teacher).

FOLDES, DESZO, DR. (Councillor Buda Pest).

FRIEDLANDER, LOUIS (German Classic Scholar).

GARTENHAUS, REV. JACOB (Baptist Evangelist and author of Tracts for Jews, U. S.)

GINZBURG, REV. DR. CHRISTIAN (Massoretic Scholar).

GITTEL, REV. I. (Presby. minister and missionary, U. S.)

GOLD-LEVIN, REV. A. P. D. D. DILLITT.

GORODISHZ, REV. P. (F. R. G. S.) Poland.

GOTTHEIL, REV. P. E. (Brother of Rabbi Gottheil, of Temple Emmanuel), New York City.

GREENBAUM, REV. E. S. (Ep. Clergyman and missionary, Canada).

GREGORY, BAR-HEBRAUS (Bishop in the Eastern Church and a Philosophical and Theological Writer).

HELMUTH, RT. REV. J., D.D., D.C.L. (Bishop of Huron, Canada).

HERSCHELL, SIR C. L. (Great Astronomer).

HERSCHELL, LORD (Lord Chancellor of England).

HERSCHELL, REV. RIDLEY, D.D. (Founder of the British Society and father of Lord Herschell, Lord Chancellor of England).

HERSHON, DON JUAN (a Converted Rabbi and later Professor of Oriental Languages in the University of Madrid, Spain).

HILLEL, Son of Judah the Second, a Patriarch of Tiberias.

ISAACS, HON. GERARD (Son of Baron Reading of England).

JACOB, of Kefar, Neuburaya (mentioned in the Talmud) converted in the Fourth Century.

JACOBI, REV. B. F., D.D. (Founder of Methodism in St. Louis, Mo.).

JUSTIN, 118 A. D.

KOHN, RT. REV. THEODORE, D.D. (Archbishop of Olmutz, Austria).

LANDSMANN, REV. J. I. (Hebrew Scholar, Poland).

LICHTENSTEIN, RABBI ISAAC (District Rabbi of Tapio, Szele, Hungary).

LICHTENSTEIN, RABBI L. (Hungary).

LEVERTOFF, REV. PAUL D. D. (Lambeth).

LEVISON, SIR LEON (Writer and Missionary, Knighted by King George for activities in behalf of suffering Jews in Russia).

LEVY, REV. MARK JOHN.

LEWEK, REV. J. R. (Veteran Jewish Missionary, U. S.)

LOWENTHAL, REV. ISIDOR (Translator of the New Testament into Pushto; Missionary Martyr).

MACHLIN, REV. A. B. (Baptist minister, former Socialist, U. S.).

MENDELSSOHN, SORELL (Youngest Daughter of Moses Mendelssohn, the Philosopher).

MENDELSSOHN, DOROTHEA (born of the Famous Mendelssohn Family).

MENDELSSOHN, FELIX B. (Great Musician).

MONTEFIORE, LYDIA (Aunt of Sir Moses Montefiore).

MORRIS, REV JUDAH (Professor of Hebrew at Harvard).

NEANDER, PROF. AUGUSTUS, D.D. (The Church Historian, Berlin, Germany).

NEWGEWIRTZ, REV. D. J. (Ep. Clergyman and Veteran Missionary, Canada.)

NEWMAN, REV. ELIAS (Presbyterian Minister and Veteran Missionary).

OFFENBACH, JACQUES (Composer).

PASHA, EMIN (Explorer).

PELTZ, REV. JACOB (Presbyterian Minister, Exect. Sec. Hebrew Christian Alliance, U. S.)

PHILIPI, REV. DR. FREDERICH A. (Lutheran Theologian, Germany).

RABINOWITCH, JOSEPH (Lawyer and Hebrew-Christian Leader, Russia).

REICH, MAX (Minister Society of Friends and Author).

ROHOLD, S.B., F.R.G.S. (Missionary, Died in 1931).

RUBINSTEIN, NIKOLAI (Russian Pianist, Brother of Anton Rubinstein).

SALKINSON, E. C. (Hebrew Poet).

SALKINSON, REV. ISAAC, D.D. (Translator of the New Testament into Hebrew).

SAPHIR, REV. DR. ADOLPH (Famous Presbyterian Minister "Mighty in the Scriptures," London, England).

SCHAPIRO, B. A. M. (Hebrew Scholar and Author).

SHERESHEWSKI, RT. REV. S.L.J., D.D. (The Translator of the Bible into Chinese).

SIGEL, M. (Missionary).

STAHL, PROF. FRIEDERICH J. (Jurist and Publicist.)

STEINER, DR. E. (Professor, Author and Lecturer, U. S.)

TORRES, LOUIS DE (First White Man to reach American Soil).

WERTHEIMER, MAX PH. D., (Ex-Rabbi).

ZACKER, REV. J. L. (Anglican Clergyman, U. S.)

ZECKHAUSEN, REV. HARRY, M. D. (Lutheran minister, U. S.)

ZEIDMAN, REV. MORRIS, B. D.

To this very short list could be added hundreds more of the eminent Jews who have accepted the Messiahship of Jesus of Nazareth, but lack of space forbids.